Disruptive, Stubborn, Out of Control

of related interest

No Fighting, No Biting, No Screaming
How to Make Behaving Positively Possible for People with Autism and Other Developmental Disabilities
Bo Hejlskov Elvén
ISBN 978 1 84905 126 2
eISBN 978 0 85700 322 5

Sulky, Rowdy, Rude?
Why kids really act out and what to do about it
Bo Hejlskov Elvén and Tina Wiman
ISBN 978 1 78592 213 8
eISBN 978 1 78450 492 2

Confused, Angry, Anxious?
Why working with older people in care really can be difficult, and what to do about it
Bo Hejlskov Elvén, Charlotte Agger, and Iben Ljungmann
ISBN 978 1 78592 215 2
eISBN 978 1 78450 494 6

Frightened, Disturbed, Dangerous?
Why working with patients in psychiatric care can be really difficult, and what to do about it
Bo Hejlskov Elvén and Sophie Abild McFarlane
ISBN 978 1 78592 214 5
eISBN 978 1 78450 493 9

Disruptive, Stubborn, Out of Control?

Why kids get confrontational in the classroom, and what to do about it

Bo Hejlskov Elvén

Jessica Kingsley *Publishers*
London and Philadelphia

First published in 2017
by Jessica Kingsley Publishers
73 Collier Street
London N1 9BE, UK
and
400 Market Street, Suite 400
Philadelphia, PA 19106, USA

www.jkp.com

Copyright © Bo Hejlskov Elvén 2017

Library of Congress Cataloging in Publication Data
A CIP catalog record for this book is available from the Library of Congress

British Library Cataloguing in Publication Data
A CIP catalogue record for this book is available from the British Library

ISBN: 978 1 78592 212 1
eISBN: 978 1 78450 490 8

Printed and bound in Great Britain

MIX
Paper from
responsible sources
FSC® C013056

Contents

Introduction

One of the questions I am asked most often when I talk to members of staff in schools is: 'How can I teach when my pupils behave in this way – should they really be allowed to carry on like this?' I have been asked this question repeatedly over the 15 years that I have worked as a psychologist in schools, through employment in child and youth psychiatry, as a school psychologist, or as a consultant.

What I find interesting is that the teacher asking this question is expressing powerlessness regarding the pupil's behaviour that is of no help to the pupil in handling the situation. The teacher simply has no method to use in handling the pupil's behaviour.

Everybody studying for school vocations learns different things. As a teacher, you will of course have learnt a great deal about the subjects you teach. Perhaps you have also studied some teaching theory and how knowledge is acquired and taught to others. And possibly you have learnt about how children develop, and about the major psychological theories.

Whatever your education, after completing your studies you will have started working. Maybe you were then surprised by how little you had actually learnt about your job. Perhaps your education taught you how to help your pupils learn by working with textbooks on maths, but not how to make them take their books out of their bags. When your pupils then actually don't take out their books, you suddenly realise that certain things are missing in your education.

This book is about how you as a teacher can work with behaviour that challenges at school. How you can think, act, and approach pupils who exhibit behaviour that challenges in a way that works, so that you can take responsibility for them meeting the learning goals. The book is based on research about how people and children act, and on what works and what does not in school. There are no in-text references, but at the end of the book you will find more information about the research and theory on which the book is based, chapter by chapter, with suggestions for further reading.

BEHAVIOUR THAT CHALLENGES AT SCHOOL DISRUPTS TEACHING

At school we most often focus on teaching, and behaviour that challenges becomes something that disrupts the teaching; it hinders us from doing our job, and perhaps we think that someone else should take care of it. Either the pupils themselves (who should behave), the pupils' parents (who should make sure the pupils behave, though it is unclear how), or the school principal and politicians (who should make sure that such pupils are not included in ordinary classes).

Thinking in this way seldom helps, however; more likely it increases the feeling of powerlessness. A solution many of us resort to in such situations is to start telling the pupils off sharply – which is rarely a good solution since it rather increases the opposition between the pupils and us.

There is danger in merely handling behaviour that challenges to the best of your ability, without knowing how you actually should act, because you risk using methods that don't work. One wonders why schools are reluctant to have an amateur teaching the pupils maths, yet strangely enough often let teachers with no professional knowledge of behaviour that challenges handle such behaviour. It is therefore not very surprising that things sometimes go haywire.

INCREASED KNOWLEDGE AND EFFECTIVE, PROFESSIONAL MANAGEMENT

This book describes how the school as an institution and you as a teacher, based on scientific evidence, can manage behaviour that challenges in an effective and professional way. It also presents a method, called the low-arousal approach, which can help you significantly improve everyday life when this kind of situation occurs at your school. Regarding the teacher's approach, research has shown that if we are to effectively reduce behaviour that challenges in our pupils, we need to start by changing our own attitude. The method I describe illustrates, among other things, what the right attitude might be.

Perhaps you who have chosen to read this book have come to realise that the methods you usually use at school are inadequate for challenging situations. In that case, I hope it will help you create the openness needed to use methods beyond 'common sense' (an expression many use when there are no good arguments to support what they are doing) and dare to try thinking and acting differently. If you dare do this, you will most likely discover an effective way of working and get good results in the meetings with your pupils with behaviour that challenges. But it will require you to be both flexible and open!

DISPOSITION

The book consists of three parts. The first is divided into 11 chapters, each of which is based on a principle that is illustrated using a real-life situation derived from my work in schools. All of the principles are part of an approach called the *low-arousal approach*, which is based on research on managing behaviour that challenges. The low-arousal approach consists of both an attitude and a number of practical methods, with a focus on managing and reducing behaviour that challenges in everyday life. The attitude is best described by the principles on which the book is based, and the methods are woven in throughout the book, in the adjustment of demands, management of conflicts, and management of physical violence. Some of the principles are very remote from the ways in which we usually think in schools. Perhaps also remote from the way in which you, if you are a parent, deal with your children. Some of the principles have been formulated by other psychologists, and this is clarified where the principle is described; others I have formulated myself.

The second part of the book describes three case scenarios. Each scenario is introduced using a real-life situation which is discussed in the light of the principles handled in the first part of the book. The examples are then coupled to suggested action plans. By looking at the scenarios in this way, you can understand what is actually happening, what you need to change, and how you can make a potential strategy for managing such situations if they occur again. Feel free to use them as the basis for discussions in your teaching team on how you can work with behaviour that challenges at your school.

The third part includes study materials and further reading.

Part 1

Principles

1

Always Identify the One With the Problem

GEORGE

George plays football during the break; he's good at football. Oliver tackles him so hard that he falls down. He hurts his leg and grazes his arm. Soon afterwards, the break is over and they go in to the classroom. Oliver laughs at George's sore arm. George turns bright red in the face and comes at Oliver with raised fists. The teacher, Peter, takes hold of George's arm to stop him, but catches just where the sore is and George shouts loudly. Peter keeps his grip, however, and says: 'Calm down now!' George twists free and runs out of the classroom with only socks on his feet, away from the school. Peter doesn't know what to do; the traffic is dangerous, he thinks, the pupils have to be at school, and after all, it is the school that has the responsibility. If George is hit by a car the school will be in trouble.

The next day Peter invites George's parents to a meeting where he tells them that, yet again, George's behaviour during this incident has caused a lot of trouble for the school. The school had to send out three members of staff to look for him. They were busy for almost an hour, until George's mum called from work and asked what had happened. It turned out that George had run the two miles to her workplace and told her that Peter was an idiot.

Peter lets George's parents know that if George runs away again during school hours, an evaluation will have to be made of whether he can remain in the regular class.

IT'S THE SCHOOL'S PROBLEM, NOT THE PUPILS' PROBLEM

The principle 'Always identify the one with a problem' is simple. As teachers, we often assume that our own impression of things is the correct one. If we think someone's behaviour is problematic, we most often think that everyone else feels the same way. But this is not automatically true. In the example above, a difficult situation ends with George running off, something that George's teacher sees as a big problem. George himself rather sees it as a solution, which means that there is not really any incentive for him to change his behaviour. He is handling a difficult situation in a way that seems good to him. For the teachers at George's school there's a problem, however. When they don't know where George is, they can't take responsibility for him.

If the school assumes in this situation that George has a behaviour problem, things will get difficult. The school will then want him to change his behaviour, whereas George, since he does not think he has a problem, will not be inclined to exchange his solution for what seems a poorer alternative.

In this situation, the school must instead find a way to ensure that the same thing doesn't happen again. But this requires that the school's motivation to change the situation is greater than George's. In addition, the teachers' ability to change the situation must be greater than George's. They are adults and professionals. George is only a child.

APRIL

April thinks maths is difficult. She's meant to be learning division and just doesn't understand. She has trouble concentrating in class – there's too much going on. In order to screen out some of the input, she puts on her winter jacket and pulls up the hood. April's teacher, Violet, asks her to take off her jacket, but she doesn't want to do that. Violet tells her a couple of times, and when April doesn't take off her hood, Violet pulls it back herself. April waits for a while, then pulls it up again while Violet is looking the other way.

In April's case too, there is a reason for her behaviour. She wants to concentrate, but Violet, who pulls back the hood of her jacket even though April wants it up, doesn't understand this. April is a resourceful girl, however; she's patient and pulls up the hood again after a while. The one who has a problem with April having her hood up is Violet. April's problem is that the classroom is too noisy and that Violet is pulling her hood off. This means that there are two different problems and therefore also two different solutions. To expect April to understand and solve Violet's problem in this situation is probably not the school's first-choice option.

THE PUPILS CAN'T SOLVE THE SCHOOL'S PROBLEMS

A theme running throughout this book is how we who work in schools can come to grips with the different problems we experience. It is therefore extremely important to point out from the very start that the problems I bring up are those that teachers consider problems. The book is therefore primarily about what you and your colleagues can do to solve the school's problems yourselves, not what the pupils can do to solve them. Most pupils are quite good at solving their own problems. Maybe they don't always do it with methods that the school likes, and sometimes their solutions end up with the school suddenly having problems that need to be solved. It is then important to be aware that you, as a teacher, are the one with the greatest responsibility for solving the problems. To repeat, you are the professional, not the pupils. Society needs the school to take care of its own problems. Nobody else can or will do it. The responsibility is clearly on the teachers and on the school leadership. And this is good. Only by taking responsibility can we solve the problems we meet.

Summary

In school, behaviour that challenges are often interpreted as if it is the pupil who has a problem. In reality, however, it is often you as a teacher who sees the pupil's behaviour as problematic. The pupils themselves seldom see their 'problem' as a problem, which means that they don't automatically have any motivation to change their behaviour. You must understand that the responsibility rather lies on you and your colleagues, and that you need to be highly motivated to change the current situation in order to stop the behaviour that challenges from being repeated.

2

Kids Do Well If They Can

PAUL

Paul is in fifth grade. The school he goes to is having a Viking theme for two weeks. Paul has been having a hard time sitting still during these weeks but thinks it's been great fun making Viking weapons and doing Viking wrestling. By Thursday of the second week he has written four lines for his presentation on Viking weapons. His teacher, Susanna, says that he needs to be finished by the following day. On Thursday after lunch the whole class is going to watch the film *The 13th Warrior*. Paul says he doesn't want to watch any damn shitty movie – he'd rather wrestle.

So Susanna says: 'I want you to give the film 20 minutes. If you don't like it by then you can go, but you must first watch for 20 minutes.' Paul agrees, but has a hard time concentrating. It takes eight minutes before Susanna has all the cables in place and the film session can start. Meanwhile, Paul keeps on talking about how he doesn't want to watch a shitty movie, he wants to wrestle instead. After watching about 30 seconds of the movie he says: 'Damn shitty movie. I want to wrestle. Are you coming, Jonah?' Susanna points out: 'You haven't watched for 20 minutes yet. Sit down.'

Paul goes, but Susanna stops Jonah who's about to follow Paul, and he sits down again. After a minute Paul comes back into the room and asks in a loud and clear voice why Jonah isn't coming. Susanna replies: 'Since you didn't watch for 20 minutes you can't wrestle. Either sit down and watch the film or go to the group room and work on your presentation on weapons. You decide.'

Paul tries one more time to get Jonah to come with him, but Jonah is already captivated by the movie and doesn't want to come. Susanna then takes Paul by the arm and tries to lead him out of the classroom. Paul shouts, 'Let go of me, bitch!', runs past her into the classroom, and grabs Jonah – who asks him to let go. Paul then runs out of the classroom and into the library where he pushes over some books. After this he runs out into the schoolyard and starts banging on the windows of the classroom where the others are watching the film.

ABILITIES, DEMANDS, AND EXPECTATIONS

The principle 'Kids do well if they can' was formulated by the American psychologist Ross W. Greene. The principle is actually very simple: if a child behaves well it's because he can. Accordingly, if a child isn't behaving well, it's because he isn't able to. Then the people around him need to start looking at what demands and expectations are reasonable to place on the child, considering his abilities. In Paul's case, Susanna has demands and expectations relating to several different abilities that Paul would need in the different stages of the chain of events described.

We can start with the abilities that are necessary for Paul to handle working with a theme, where the structure, of course, is different to that in the normal school day.

Among other things, theme weeks make demands on Paul's ability to structure his time. On normal school days, the schedule runs on as usual and he doesn't need to keep track of much by himself. During the theme weeks, on the other hand, he has to plan his time, and he's also meant to prepare a presentation on a topic that has to do with the Viking theme. He has chosen the topic of weapons but hasn't got very far by the second-last day of the theme period; in fact his presentation is hardly even started. Probably the lack of structure has led to an increased level of stress for Paul even before the situation with the movie starts.

On top of this, Paul is expected to be able to change his mind, and exchange his own wishes for something that Susanna wants him to do. Paul wants to wrestle, and the demand that he must watch a movie instead makes him upset. On normal school days he might have been able to handle this differently. But just as for so many of us, the stressful situation makes Paul less flexible, and he has trouble readjusting rapidly. And when it takes time for Susanna to get the film going, his restlessness increases. The ability to wait is about stamina, and Paul's stamina in this situation is fairly low. He gets more and more impatient.

When the movie finally starts, he sees two people dressed in white Arabic caftans walking up to a big tent, conversing. And since Paul at the moment is interested in Viking weapons and wrestling, and not in men wearing caftans, the scene is unexpected and makes no sense. This is the final straw. He tries to get Jonah to come with him, but when he notices that Jonah isn't following him, he comes back into the classroom. Susanna then gives him the choice of either seeing the film or working on his presentation. In Paul's head, though, the only option is wrestling, and he can't readjust so quickly. To work on his presentation instead is far too much to demand; he can neither structure his work nor envisage the final product.

When Susanna takes hold of him it becomes too much. He can no longer navigate, but resorts to a behaviour that helps him manage the situation by getting attention, and being seen and affirmed. Since Paul no longer can handle the stress by himself he needs affirmation that he exists in order to calm down. He gets this by shouting abuse, pushing over books, and banging on the windows. Not all pupils have such a need for affirmation in difficult situations, but some do.

In all this, Paul's inability to understand the consequences of his behaviour shines through. Like approximately 10 per cent of the general population, Paul simply can't see where his actions will lead. He surfs through the situation as it unfolds, on a wave over which he has no control.

All in all, we can conclude that, in the situation above, Paul has difficulties in structuring, planning and executing, restraining impulses, readjusting quickly, predicting the consequences of his actions, and controlling his affect without help.

CHARACTERISTICS AND NORMAL DISTRIBUTION

Paul is not a child with a diagnosis. His abilities lie within the normal distribution for pupils in the regular school. In Paul's class there are another two or three pupils who function in the same way. The things they have difficulty with are different, however. In this particular situation, it was the demands and expectations on Paul's abilities that overwhelmed him.

Practically all human characteristics show a normal distribution in the general population. This applies to characteristics such as height, weight, talent, attentiveness, ability to structure, ability to learn through reading, ability to wait, social abilities, and numerous other things. The normal distribution is often illustrated as in Figure 2.1.

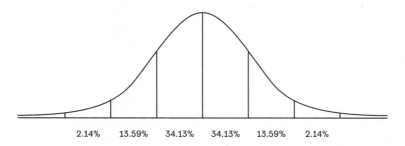

2.14%   13.59%   34.13%   34.13%   13.59%   2.14%

Figure 2.1 The normal distribution curve

The figure can be seen as a group of people placed on a line based on a given characteristic, such as height, with the shortest to the left and the tallest to the right. The great majority will be in the middle – that is, those with normal height. The figure illustrates that most people's characteristics lie around the average, regardless of the characteristic chosen. The further you move from the average, regardless of direction, the fewer people you will find. This is easy to understand when thinking of height, but exactly the same thing applies for the abilities that the school situation demands in Paul's case. If a pupil falls too far below the average for any of these abilities, the risk (or possibility) that they will receive a diagnosis increases. There is a gradual transition between diagnosis and the normal area, however, which in a normal class means that there will be some pupils who can handle a theme week very well, some who handle it well, some who handle it fairly well, and a few who will have major problems when the normal school day is replaced by something new with different demands.

CHILDREN'S RESOURCES AND ABILITIES DIFFER

That children's resources and abilities vary is a central theme that runs throughout this book. When we discuss behaviour that challenges in school, it's about which children are equipped to handle the demands that the school makes and which are not. The reasons why a pupil may be unable to live up to demands and expectations may originate in a great number of different factors, which vary from pupil to pupil and from situation to situation. They may, for example, relate to the pupil's ability in regulating affect (calming down or remaining calm), planning and executing, controlling impulses, or being flexible, but may also relate to talent and stress situations as well as to relationships with adults in the school, or security in the class.

But what we are not going to discuss here is the desire to behave well or the quality of the parents' upbringing. There are several reasons for this that I will develop further later on in the book. We will follow Greene's principle because research has shown that if you start from the premise that 'Kids do well if they can' then you become more effective in your work. We will examine this more closely in the next chapter. But first we will take a look at what it means for daily work with the pupils' behaviour.

BEHAVIOUR THAT CHALLENGES
– PART OF EVERYDAY LIFE

There will always be situations at school where things go wrong. Behaviours that challenge are not really a deviation from the normal. It is a part of everyday life – even if it is a part that seems difficult. Every time a situation at school goes out of control, we should sit down and think about what went wrong. If we then look at the different stages of the situation's development, we will very likely be able to identify happenings or factors where our demands on the pupil were too high. If we look in the right way. If instead we only look for what the pupils should have done instead of what they did, we will have problems next time we end up in a similar situation.

OUR OWN BEHAVIOUR AND OUR OWN EXPECTATIONS

So in order to understand what the problem is, we need to look at our own behaviour and our own expectations of a pupil's abilities, and compare them with the pupil's real abilities. If a pupil's behaviour in a given situation is not functioning well, we will most likely realise that this is due to our own failings. This may be difficult to accept, but that's how it is. Much is required of us in order to see our own role in the pupil's behaviour. At the same time it is absolutely imperative for us to do so if the situation is not to be repeated over and over again. We must remember that all the pupil's behaviour takes place as an interaction with the surroundings, either directly with us or with the surroundings within our influence.

DEMANDS THAT ARE TOO HIGH

In my first job as a school psychologist I wondered why, in the junior primary school classes, the lesson after the lunch break was generally used to discuss conflicts that had broken out during the break. The school's assignment was to teach, yet here they were using at least one lesson every day to discuss conflicts between the pupils. In my view, this was an enormous waste of teaching time. Conflicts during breaks happen because the breaks place demands that are too high on the pupils' different abilities: their ability to structure, their ability to control impulses, or their social abilities. After all, as Greene says, the pupils do their best. So the reason must lie in the demands made on them by the surroundings.

If a conflict arises during a break that requires us to use teaching time to sort it out, we should immediately make a plan for how we can avoid it happening again. But what form should a break have in order for the risk of conflict to be reduced? Should perhaps not all the children have a break at the same time? Should there be more teachers outside? Should we agree with the pupils on what they are going to do before the break starts? Or should we ask the three pupils with the greatest need for this what they are thinking of doing during the break, in order to create some structure in their minds and avoid them just going out and seeing where something is happening?

I work with several schools where break activities are agreed on for lower primary school classes and for some pupils in the middle classes. This takes five minutes of lesson time before the long breaks and saves 45 minutes of conflict resolution afterwards. But above all, it reduces demands on the pupils' abilities and gives them a much better day, where it is easier for them to learn.

Think about how you handle this yourself. Ask whether you have too high demands on the pupils':

- *Ability to calculate cause and effect in complex situations.* This is needed for them to predict the consequences of their own actions, but also to envisage what will happen overall. Pupils who have problems here need schedules and structure to a higher degree than others.

- *Ability to structure, plan and carry out activities.* Many pupils are unable to form an overview of a lesson and plan how they will work, and they don't know how far they have reached in their assignments. It is then difficult to keep motivation high.

- *Ability to remember while thinking, in other words – working memory.* Some pupils are unable to remember the information they have in their heads and process it at the same time. This means you can't use oral instructions for them – you may need to write out or draw what they are meant to do.

- *Ability to restrain impulses.* Many pupils react immediately to the things that happen in a situation and simply can't stop themselves from acting when the impulse comes. Because of this you need to think about what impulses you create through your rules and through the way you treat your pupils. Remember that rules about things that are not allowed create an impulse to do just those things.

- *Stamina.* Some pupils find it much more difficult to wait than others do. The same pupils often have difficulty in doing activities that require concentration over an extended period of time.

- *Ability to be flexible or to readjust quickly.* Most pupils like it when everything goes on as usual, but some find it especially difficult to handle changes, even if they are unavoidable and you perhaps think the pupils are just being silly.

- *Social abilities, such as predicting other people's thoughts, feelings, and actions.* Some pupils have a very hard time understanding their own role in things that go wrong, and in imagining what various situations and behaviours seem like to other people. These pupils often have major problems in judging other people's intentions.

- *Resilience to stress.* The amount of stress we can handle varies. Remember that pupils' ability to handle stress at school will be reduced if they are stressed in other areas of life.

- *Ability to say 'yes'.* This may sound strange, but some pupils say 'yes' to most things in life, while others say 'no'. This is a personality factor and not something that is easy to change. But you can learn to compensate for it. If a pupil finds it difficult to say 'yes' then you must increase the pupil's feeling of participation, for example by increasing the number of choices available.

- *Ability to calm down or to remain calm – in other words, the ability to regulate affect.* This varies from person to person and increases with age. It is important to understand that this is an ability, not a matter of will. After all, no-one wants to lose control of their feelings.

SHOW CONSIDERATION WHERE NEEDED

The essence of Ross W. Greene's work is that teachers must help pupils develop abilities in areas where the demands of the school and of the teachers are too high for them. He describes this very well in the books *Lost at School* and *The Explosive Child*.

In contrast, this book is about how you as a teacher, in a simple way, can learn to handle this kind of problem in everyday life at school, without the school having to waste a lot of time and money on teaching challenging pupils within a special education framework. In my opinion, this is something that can only be achieved if the school makes the necessary adjustments so that all pupils feel that there is a place for them there, and so that they learn during the normal school day.

No-one knows for sure whether Greene's principle 'Kids who can behave, do so' is correct. But both my own experience and plenty of research indicate that following it is effective, and that's enough for me. If you think in this way, apply it in your everyday life at school, and stop to think about what abilities you are implicitly demanding, the number of conflicts will drop dramatically. As a result the pupils will learn more and your feeling of success will increase.

In the next chapter I will discuss how pupils behave when they are subjected to demands and expectations that they are unable to meet. In these situations they do what makes most sense – as in Paul's case above, to wrestle. He thereby avoids other activities that make no sense to him. There is nothing strange about this. It's how all of us act.

Summary
Kids do well if they can. If your pupils don't behave then you most likely have too high expectations of their abilities. In order to change this, you can map out the expectations you had in situations that went wrong and change them, and you can also think about which abilities the pupils are expected to have in order to live up to the demands.

3

People Always Do What Makes Sense

THE CORRIDOR

A few years ago I was at a primary school on a guidance assignment. During the coffee break, the principal said: 'We're having a lot of trouble with pupils running in the corridors. We have to have members of staff stationed in the corridors in the morning and afternoon, and we have to follow the pupils in and out at breaks in order to avoid complete chaos. The number of times we have to tell pupils off is enormous, but what is one to do?' 'How long have you had this problem?' I asked. 'Since 1967 when the school was built,' he replied. 'Then it's probably not the pupils' fault,' I said. 'I think we need to go and look at the corridor.'

Sure enough, the corridor was six metres wide, six metres high, and a hundred metres long. No primary school pupils can walk slowly in a corridor like that – it invites you to run. Running in such a corridor is a logical action.

We solved the problem by changing the corridor. Half-walls were placed between each classroom, reaching a little further than the middle of the corridor, which slowed the pupils down considerably. Now they couldn't see a hundred metres ahead, only about ten metres. We simply changed what was understandable in the corridor.

UNDERSTANDABLE ACTIONS

Most of us try to do what makes most sense in the situation we happen to be in. There are many examples of this. Regardless of the speed limit shown on the traffic sign, for example, we tend to drive more slowly on narrow roads than on broader ones. And even slower if the road has many curves. Slowing down when the road gets narrower is the most logical thing to do. In the same way, it is a completely logical and understandable action for a preschool child to jump into an inviting puddle. To choose anything else requires an active impulse control.

In a similar way, it is fully understandable for Paul in the previous chapter to leave a situation that is placing too high demands on his abilities. In fact it is the most important and sensible thing to do.

This is not about understanding. I often find that teachers think they can improve the behaviour of their pupils by talking to them. I don't think so. Saying 'But surely you must understand...' is not the right way to go when the pupils don't have the ability to calculate cause and effect in complex situations. Or when they don't understand why they should go to school.

'WHY DO YOU GO TO SCHOOL?'

I often amuse myself at the start of school by asking pupils why they should go to school. They all answer: 'So that I can learn to read, write, and count.' They understand. Later in fourth grade when I ask them whether they have learnt to read, write, and count, they usually say 'yes'. If I then ask them 'Then why are you still at school?' they are usually totally stumped. They have lost the understanding of why they go to school. But still they go. Perhaps because it makes sense in another way.

I think this has to do with several different factors. Partly that everyone else goes to school, and that ten-year-old children want to be like everyone else. Partly that children's parents think they should go to school, and as a ten-year-old you want to do what's expected of you. Also, your friends go to school, and of course you want to be with them. A factor that can cause a little uncertainty is relationships with the adults at school. For a pupil who has good relationships with the adults, this will be a powerful factor in helping the child go to school. For a pupil who does not have such a relationship, it can work the other way around. Another factor can be the affirmation that good pupils get at school. But this of course only applies to the quarter of the pupils who are the highest achievers. For the lowest-achieving quarter, it instead becomes a negative factor.

All these factors in combination are usually enough to keep pupil attendance high in primary school. In early secondary school grades, though, the pupils suddenly don't want to be like everyone else, and don't want to do what their parents expect them to do. Then the only factors left that can keep non-attendance at school low are friends and relationships with the adults – that is to say, if the pupil is not already among the highest achievers. Unfortunately, relationships with adults are less prioritised in secondary school, so in practice, friends are often the only remaining sense factor for going to school. If then a pupil has weak social abilities and has difficulty in handling the complex social interaction that secondary school entails, there is a risk that absenteeism will be high. The same thing applies to pupils who manage well in social groups and therefore perhaps choose to spend the day as a group in town, rather than going to school. In all cases, it's about the pupils doing what makes sense.

Towards the middle of secondary school, some pupils suddenly understand why they are going to school, and they start talking about the careers they want to pursue. But again, this is only a powerful factor for the highest-achieving quarter of the class. Unfortunately, it's not a strong enough reason for the other pupils; they can't manage to do what they should do even though they know what it is. If it was so simple that understanding in itself was enough to lead to a change in behaviour, then we wouldn't have any smokers and everyone would have normal weight.

Strangely enough, the most common intervention for absenteeism from school is for the teacher to simply have a talk with the pupil about how important it is to go to school. This means relying on the pupil's understanding, which probably constitutes a very small part of why kids go to school. The most commonly used method by far is appealing – that is, appealing to the pupil's understanding. Unfortunately, this seldom has any effect.

The reason many of us resort to appealing is probably that we also do what makes most sense, without thinking very much about what is effective. It is then important to remember that most of it came from favourable circumstances for going to school, and that this is one of the reasons why we chose to make a career in school. The pupils we have problems with are therefore different to us. So just because it might have helped if someone talked to us when we were at school, there is no guarantee that it will help the pupils who we have problems with.

RULES THAT DON'T MAKE SENSE
ARE DIFFICULT TO FOLLOW

One of the most common forms of behaviour that challenges at school is that pupils don't obey the school rules. When I talk to teachers about this, most of them seem to think that of course everyone should follow the rules. It's also not unusual that institution of a new rule is the first action taken when a problem arises. In these situations I usually ask the teachers whether they themselves follow all the rules in society. Over and over again it turns out that they don't. As humans, we follow the rules we understand. We have difficulty in following rules that don't make sense.

That it is difficult to follow rules that don't make sense can easily be demonstrated by looking at traffic. For example, people driving small cars more often keep to the speed limit than those with bigger cars, where the speed is not as noticeable. It is understandable to drive at 110 km/h on a highway if your engine sounds like it's labouring and there is a lot of noise from the road and wind, but not if the car is running smoothly and quietly. And many people ignore red lights at pedestrian crossings if there is no traffic. It makes no sense to stand and wait when it's completely safe to cross the road. In the same way, pupils follow the rules that make sense and cheat with those that don't.

CAP ON INDOORS

A good example of a rule that makes no sense to many pupils is that in most schools you are not allowed to wear a cap or hat indoors. This makes perfect sense for most adults, who have grown up not wearing a cap or hat indoors. For them, there is nothing strange about this – you probably think that a cap or hat is primarily a practical item of clothing, with a focus on keeping warm. However, for today's young people, things are not so straightforward: for them a hat or cap is more about how they look, and their identity. Even for the younger teachers, having a hat or cap on indoors makes sense. So the rules have been changed in some schools.

The important thing here is to be aware of the fact that for pupils who see their hat as an expression of identity, it doesn't make sense to take your hat off indoors. In a school that requires pupils to be hat- and cap-free when indoors, the staff will have to remind and nag every day. And this comes with a price. The pupils will think that the adults who are always nagging about their hats are idiots. And who can learn anything from idiots?

I would go as far as to say that pupils not being allowed to have a hat or cap on while indoors contributes to some pupils gaining lower grades than they otherwise would. The conflicts that such a rule leads to can sabotage the alliance that is the foundation of all learning. Not for all pupils, but for the small minority for whom the hat or cap is an important part of their identity.

The school has a whole row of other culture-associated rules, such as not being allowed to chew gum in class. I was involved in a little experiment in a school in Sweden a few years ago: the teachers stopped nagging at pupils who chewed gum, which resulted in gum chewing actually declining to some extent. The amount of gum under the desks also fell by 75 per cent. Why? Because the pupils no longer needed to stick their gum under the desk to avoid getting caught by the teachers. When the teachers later evaluated the experiment, they reached the conclusion that nagging about chewing gum was much more disruptive to teaching than the gum chewing itself.

SHORTCUTS

If the school wants to work with sense as an educational principle, there are a lot of shortcuts available. It is always good to start with the physical framework, for example. Building away behaviour that challenges is often the cheapest intervention there is. A school simply should not have corridors that invite you to run, if this is dangerous and a cause of unrest. Or have cramped spaces where pupils have to line up and fuss can easily start. It would do away with lots of problem situations if schools were built so that queues could never form. It would also mean reduced staffing costs and give you and your colleagues time to do what you were employed to do – teach. The number of square metres per pupil should also be increased; this would reduce the level of both noise and conflict. A door that doesn't slam but quietly glides shut creates peace and quiet. Good lighting reduces stress and increases learning. And perhaps most important of all: to strive for a calm environment in the large central halls; they are most often an invitation to fuss, harassment, and bullying. Put a library there instead, for example.

Another shortcut to making the behaviour we prefer making sense is by increasing predictability for the pupils. Many of them have no trouble working quietly if they have an overview of what they are going to do and for how long they are going to do it. So if you put a lesson plan on the board before each lesson, behaviour that challenges such as rowdiness and pupils leaving their seats will be considerably reduced. The plan helps the pupils to get an overview of the lesson and the work that needs to be done. But you must also remember to cross out the activities that have been completed. A couple of pupils in every class may need a printed copy of the lesson plan on their desk; this is something I have seen the value of many times. As one teacher put it: 'I always plan my class anyway, so it's no problem to print out copies of my plan for the two pupils who need it the most.' There may also be pupils who need fixed assignments in order to make working more understandable. If 90 per cent of a class can handle group work, perhaps the other 10 per cent need six concrete questions to answer if they are to gain any benefit from the lesson.

The same applies to breaks. Many pupils have no problem navigating through an unstructured break, while others need to know what they are going to do. Some pupils solve this by always doing the same thing at all breaks, such as playing football or cards. Football has a tendency, though, to place demands that are too high on some pupils' ability to cope with unexpected happenings (like losing the game or the ball). Football, in other words, is a break activity where certain problems could be reduced considerably if a teacher took responsibility. In my experience, a playing referee best achieves the authority needed to reduce conflicts on the football field. It creates an understandable structure for pupils who have difficulty navigating socially.

Once again: pupils' resources and abilities differ. Behaviour that challenges arise when we expect them to have abilities that they don't actually possess.

Summary

Pupils always do what makes most sense in a given situation. In order to understand behaviour that challenges at school you therefore need to think about how the pupils' behaviour makes sense to them. If you want to reduce behaviour that challenges, you need to create the necessary conditions for the pupils to behave by making the behaviour you prefer make sense.

4

Those Who Take Responsibility Can Make a Difference

ANDREW

Andrew is ten years old. During a break he gets into an argument with another boy about who had the swing first. The argument develops into a fight, and Andrew gets in such a hard punch that the other boy falls against a concrete edge and knocks out a tooth. A teacher on playground duty intervenes, pulls away Andrew, and tells him off. Andrew twists free, calls the teacher a damn idiot, and runs away. He keeps to himself for the rest of the day, but goes home as usual at the end of the day.

In the evening Andrew's teacher phones home to Andrew's mum and tells her what happened. Andrew's mum asks: 'Why are you calling me about this?' The teacher answers: 'So you can tell him that this is not the way to behave. It is not OK to hit other pupils, and you need to talk about this at home so that he understands. You also need to tell him that one doesn't call teachers damn idiots. If he does it again we will consider suspending him for a week.'

WHOSE RESPONSIBILITY IS IT?

The principle 'Those who take responsibility can make a difference' was formulated by the American psychologist Bernard Weiner. It received enormous circulation in occupational psychology around the turn of the millennium, when concepts such as having an influence on one's work situation became important in reducing sick leave and improving well-being at work.

In the example above it starts to get difficult when the school thinks that Andrew's mother should have a conversation with her son about what happened, and that the result of this conversation should be that it doesn't happen again. It means, you see, that either Andrew himself must ensure that it doesn't happen again, or else his mother must do so. And if it does happen again, the school will be at a loss as to what to do. If the school's way of handling a problem is to place the responsibility on the pupil or the pupil's parents, then the school becomes powerless. It then has no possibility of solving the problem. And powerless teachers with no possibility to make a difference are a huge problem. This is not the right way to go about reducing behaviour that challenges at school, even if at first sight it may seem the most sensible thing to do. Teachers, too, do what makes most sense in the situation, even if it is not the optimal thing to do.

We can use a metaphor to understand the principle a little better:

Many of us get a parking ticket once in a while. When you get a parking ticket you have two options:

- You can think that you parked your car in the wrong place. This will probably mean that you park somewhere else next time and avoid getting more parking tickets.

- You can think that parking attendants are idiots. The problem with this point of view is that you will not change your behaviour, which means that you will probably get another parking ticket soon. And when that happens, your view on parking attendants will be confirmed: they are indeed idiots. Which means that you will not change where you park. But you may develop a parking attendant paranoia.

When we use this metaphor in understanding the situation with Andrew we can conclude the following.

Firstly, the teacher who thinks Andrew himself is responsible for his behaviour will encounter many similar situations in the future. The teacher will experience the feeling of helplessness that comes from not being able to influence Andrew's behaviour. This means in turn that the teacher will go to school every day dreading what may happen. It may get so bad that it will depend on Andrew whether the teacher has a good day or not. Having this kind of situation at a school leads to increased sick leave and staff turnover, which in turn has negative effects on all the pupils' learning and grades.

In contrast, the teacher who decides that Andrew did his best but that the situation was too unstructured for him to navigate in, and that the concrete edge was badly placed, has the possibility to make changes to ensure that it won't happen again. Such teachers can make a difference to the situation, and by extension, to their work, which for the school will mean reduced sick leave, reduced staff turnover, and better development and learning for the pupils.

THE TEACHERS' ROLE

As a teacher, one may understandably enough often feel strong frustration in situations like the one with Andrew. When I encounter such situations as a consultant I often get questions like 'Should the pupil really be allowed to behave and talk in this way? 'and' Should there be no consequences?' I find this an interesting thing to say. First of all, of course no-one thinks it's OK for Andrew to fight or call people names. Not even Andrew. But in a difficult situation he's doing the best he can, which in this case is obviously not very good. What's done is done, however, and this is what the teachers working with Andrew need to relate to. The question they should ask themselves is how to reduce the risk that it will happen again. This is where consequences and punishment come in. Most of us think that if someone experiences a negative consequence after a given behaviour then that behaviour will decrease. Because that is how we think it is for us.

THE DIFFERENCE BETWEEN PUNISHMENT AND CONSEQUENCES THAT WORK

The difference between punishment and consequences that work has been discussed by psychologists, sociologists, and educational scientists over the years. A look at the research around this really shows only one factor that is interesting, namely that behaviour that challenges worsen if pupils feel that a rebuke or imposed consequence is a punishment. It doesn't matter what is actually said or done – what matters is how it's experienced by the pupil. The consequences that most of us remember and that we think were helpful are not those we saw as punishment.

Specifically when it comes to the consequences of punishment, we know quite a lot, for example that:

- Punishment most often leads to a feeling of being unfairly treated. The pupils often say 'What? It wasn't just me!' when a teacher intervenes and metes out punishment. When a pupil feels unfairly treated by a teacher, this hurts the relationship with the teacher, sometimes called the pedagogical alliance, which is central to the pupil's learning.

- In the long term, punishment leads to an increase in the behaviour being punished, rather than the opposite. This is true both on the societal and individual level. This is the reason why first-time offenders often are given conditional sentences. Non-conditional sentences for first-time offenders are associated with a dramatic increase in crime relapse compared with conditional sentences.

- Punishment may give legitimacy to behaviour that challenges. Research by the behavioural economists Uri Gneezy and Aldo Rustichini has shown that you can double the number of children left at day-care centres at closing time by instituting a punishment (in the form of a fine) for those arriving late to pick up their children. The reason is that the punishment takes away our bad conscience. This effect goes both ways. If you know what something is going to cost, there is a risk that you will judge the value of the action to be greater than the price you must pay – and you will then perform the action. It is also possible that after receiving punishment for an action, you no longer feel it necessary to think that you did something wrong – after all, you took your punishment! This is something you often see with pupils who are regularly sent out of the classroom if they cause a disturbance – they start disturbing on purpose in order to miss a class they think is boring.

We humans have varying tendencies to punish people around us, something I usually call the de Quervain effect, after the Swiss researcher Dominique de Quervain. In 2005 he published an interesting article where he and some colleagues examined two questions: partly whether differences could be seen depending on who was doing the punishing; and partly why we do it at all. They arrived at some interesting answers, among them that people have varying tendencies to punish, and that this can be predicted by measuring activity in the part of the brain known as the dorsal striatum. The greater the activity, the greater the tendency to punish. This is interesting in itself, not least in understanding why some of you may find it easier to accept this part of the book than others. It is also interesting because the researchers found that people who punished others received a personal feeling of reward. It simply felt good. Even if the person lost something by punishing the other, they experienced a feeling of competence and justice.

A researcher who has speculated more about this is the American anthropologist Robert Boyd. He suggests that, in prehistoric times, groups that threw out individuals that spoiled things for the flock or the village survived better than those that did not. In his opinion, this is why humans have developed a reward effect from punishing others.

In most of the world today, however, we have a school intended for everyone. This means that the school cannot resort to an evolutionary mechanism with a focus on group survival in the Stone Age every time a pupil says something insulting. The question is not whether the pupils should be allowed to say or do whatever they want to, but rather how you can make sure that they don't do it again. This leads us back to the chapter on the principle 'Kids do well if they can'. What is it in Andrew's situation that prevents him from behaving – why can't he handle it? How can the teachers around him change the conditions so that he succeeds better next time?

REWARDS

Since punishment and reward are two sides of the same coin, I also want to touch on rewards here. Rewards also place responsibility on the pupils.

JULIAN

Julian is 15 years old. He has difficulty getting out of bed in the mornings. His parents leave early for work, so it's up to him to make sure that he gets up and goes off to school. About three times a week he arrives a half-hour late. Both the school and his parents consider this to be a problem. Discussions are held, and together they come up with a solution: every time Julian comes to school on time, he gets a smiley. When he has collected five smileys, he gets a ticket to the cinema from his parents. Everyone thinks this is a good solution – the school, Julian, and Julian's parents.

The first week goes well. Julian is in school on time every morning. On Saturday he goes to the cinema. The second week goes just as well. Julian goes to the cinema again on Saturday. Then Monday comes.

When Julian doesn't arrive at school, not at nine, nor ten, nor eleven, his teacher phones him and asks: 'Aren't you coming today?' Julian replies: 'No, I think I'll take the day off today.' 'What about tomorrow then?' the teacher continues. Julian says: 'We'll see.' 'But then there will be no cinema ticket for the weekend,' says the teacher. Julian answers calmly: 'No, but that doesn't matter, because there aren't any good films on this weekend.'

The problem with a token economy like this is that it places the responsibility on Julian, on the pupil. And Julian willingly accepts that responsibility. But not in the way the school and parents expected. When Julian is prepared to pay the cost of not going to school, he chooses to stay at home. This is a true story. In Julian's case, this led to a tenfold increase in his absences. The reason is that rewards, just like punishments, can legitimise the pupil's feeling that it is OK to do wrong. In my experience, a token economy can render the result that the very behaviour we want to see increase actually becomes less frequent than before we started to offer rewards. The exact opposite of what we want to achieve.

Rewards also have a tendency to affect us humans in such a way that we start doing things in order to get a reward, instead of doing them because we want to, or realise that we ought to.

Some side effects of rewards and token economies are:

- *The inflation effect.* All token economies involve negotiation. We usually make an estimate of how little reward can be offered to gain the desired behaviour. If the pupil accepts the reward, then it works. But all negotiations imply that, after a while, the pupil can try to negotiate for a bigger reward. This often happens over time. There is inflation in the economy and the pupil requires greater and greater rewards for the same behaviour.

- *The diminishing satisfaction effect.* When you get your first paycheque, it's a fantastic feeling. Every subsequent time you receive your pay during the first year of work, that feeling is diminished. After a few years, you're mostly just relieved that the pay arrives at all. The joy in receiving a reward for work done diminishes over time. Maybe because when you're young, you're not sure that you are worthy of the pay. As we become more experienced, most people feel that they deserve more. I see the same effect when the work around a particular pupil is based on rewards. After a few years, inflation has increased to the point where it costs a video-game a week just to get through the day. But the reward doesn't bring joy any more, since the pupil feels that he deserves it. It's very sad to see a 13-year-old who doesn't get any joy from receiving a reward.

- *The punishment effect.* In token economies it is often described as a reward when pupils receive a star if, for example, they arrive on time. When they have earned ten stars, they can exchange them for an activity or something similar. But if they arrive late, and therefore don't get a star, they often perceive this as a punishment. Even if the teachers only see it as a missed reward. Sometimes conflicts also arise when the pupil feels that he didn't do wrong on purpose. When an unpaid reward is perceived as punishment, then the token economy won't work as intended. Because, as mentioned above, punishment does not have the positive effect that many think it does.

- *The opposition effect.* A reward is, at its core, part of a power relationship. It is the teachers who decide what should be rewarded and when the pupils have earned the reward. This places the teachers in a relationship of opposition to the pupils. Some psychologists try to avoid this by recommending that the rewards be discussed with the pupils and that they themselves be allowed to suggest rewards and when they are to be given out. This is better, but in most cases it is still the teachers who decide.

- *The behaviour-reducing effect.* The token economy is built on the idea that motivation for the behaviour we are rewarding will increase, so that we can phase out the reward after a while. This is not the case. American psychologist Edward Deci and his research group have shown, in many studies, that behaviour that is rewarded diminishes when the reward disappears. It actually diminishes to levels that are lower than before we started offering the reward. This means that we need to be careful when we use rewards. An occasional reward may be effective when, for example, a child has to go to the dentist and doesn't dare, but don't use rewards for doing homework or similar everyday activities. Because then the homework done will be reduced in the long run, when we phase out the token economy. And let's be honest: how many adults would go to work if the salary was phased out?

- *The someone-has-to-win effect.* A relationship of opposition means that someone always has to win. Either the teachers or the pupils. At the beginning teachers take it for granted that they will be the winners, but this is often opposed by the pupils. This is not so strange. No one wants to lose. But it means that the relationship between teachers and pupils suffers. This book works on the assumption that it is better to cooperate with pupils than to fight with them. And so the token economy becomes a problem. It works against cooperation because of the built-in power structure.

This of course doesn't mean that a reward is never effective. In some situations, when we really, really need the pupil to do something, of course we can offer a reward. But keep it for those situations. If we start rewarding everyday activities the side effects will prevail after quite a short time.

THE SKILL CEILING AND DISTRIBUTION OF RESPONSIBILITY

We find it easy to take responsibility when we have a good method to use. If only we know what to do and what works, then we are happy to do it. But sometimes we end up in situations where we don't have a method that works. I call this hitting the skill ceiling. When it happens, there is a tendency to immediately shift the responsibility to someone else, for example by punishing the pupil concerned (with arguments such as 'perhaps now they'll learn; after all, they have to take responsibility') or by screaming, shouting, and yelling. Perhaps we think: 'They have to behave, and if they don't understand that then I need to say it again, but louder, so that they do understand.' Or we may lay the responsibility on the principal or the politicians by saying: 'This pupil's behaviour is so bad that he shouldn't be in ordinary school. This pupil should be in a special school.'

In a class of 28 pupils there are always a few who need more support than the school is immediately able to give them.

But I think it would be fairer for the school to say that they are unable to adapt their teaching to cater for the needs of these pupils, rather than saying that the pupils don't belong in a school intended for everyone. Research has shown that a pupil of average talent will perform worse if placed in a special school or children's service compared with adapted inclusion in a normal school. This is why we prefer to include pupils with special needs. Even the other pupils perform better when those with special needs are included.

If it is said that a pupil should not go to the regular school, this is not out of consideration for the pupil's needs but rather a matter of the school's unwillingness or inability to make the adjustments needed for that pupil to manage in a normal school environment. This inability indicates that the school has reached its skill ceiling.

Another way for the school to shift the responsibility away from itself, as in the example with Andrew, is to phone the pupil's parents. If this is the only intervention the school makes, then it is probably because they don't know what else to do. Here again they have reached the skill ceiling. I sometimes see a similar tendency when teachers blame poor grades on the pupil's home environment. Instead of moving the responsibility away from the school, we must strive to change our method so that we actually succeed in doing what we are paid to do.

THE SKILL CEILING AND MUM'S METHODS

If we who work in schools are to succeed in the teaching assignment, then the school's methods must be adapted to suit the circumstances. Talking about how the pupil has difficult circumstances at home will not lead us to better fulfil our mission, but is more likely to stop us exerting ourselves.

And then we are really failing the pupil. It is true, of course, that the school's responsibility and workload increase if the pupil's home situation is detrimental to learning. But this does not mean that the requirement on the school for the pupil to succeed can be lowered.

If we are to succeed we must therefore recognise when we have hit the skill ceiling. This is perhaps one of the most important things to work with in schools. I myself usually follow a simple rule: if I am using a method my mum might have used, well, then it's probably not the right method. I simply don't work with the kind of pupils for whom my mum's methods might have been sufficient.

The reason is simple: my mum was a florist; her profession had to do with flowers. I, on the other hand, am a psychologist; I am a professional when it comes to people, but amateur when it comes to flowers. Sure, I can put together a simple bouquet, but I leave bridal bouquets and larger flower arrangements to those who know better. My mum was an amateur when it came to people. Yes, she did raise a few ordinary children, but we would not have expected her to be able to take care of children somewhat out of the ordinary. So if, as a psychologist, I use the same methods as my mum did, then I shouldn't be getting paid. In the same way that no one would pay me to arrange flowers.

This whole problem at once gets more complicated for you as a teacher. Most children are fairly ordinary, which means it wouldn't be unreasonable to think that normal ways of upbringing should work. My mum's methods didn't always work, though. She nagged at me for ten years about hanging up my jacket when I got home, for example. This was only moderately successful. Sometimes I remembered, sometimes I didn't. Only when I reached the age of 15 did it start working reliably. The reason is that most children in primary school can't go into an entrance hall, take off their jacket, choose a hook, hang up their jacket – and then still remember why they came in and what they were going to do. This requires working memory function and functions in the frontal lobe of the brain, which are not in place until the age of about 14. Possibly a little earlier in girls than boys. My mum nagged at me from the age of five until the age of 15, at which point I actually managed to do what she asked. And when it suddenly worked, she thought it was thanks to her.

My mother is excused because she was an amateur. But as teachers, or in my case a psychologist, we are professionals. We simply have to use methods that work. It is therefore extremely important that we know what works – and also that it is possible to assess whether what we are doing is having a good effect.

EINSTEIN'S PRINCIPLE (OR WAS IT HIS?)

An easy way to evaluate our methods is to use a principle that has – probably wrongly – been attributed to Albert Einstein: 'Insanity is doing the same thing over and over again and expecting a different result.' With this, one has to agree.

So a good way of recognising when we have hit the skill ceiling is to count. Have I tried this several times already? Did it work before? If not, then why is it necessary to try the same thing again? When we hit the skill ceiling we move the responsibility for the pupils' behaviour over to the pupils themselves, their parents, the principals, politicians, or others. And when we do so, we lose the ability to influence the pupils' behaviour, which means that we are going to be ineffective, sick leave will most likely increase, and the risk of stress-induced burn out will increase dramatically.

Summary

Only by accepting responsibility can you create opportunities to influence your own situation. If you think others should solve the problems that you are experiencing then you lose the ability to make a difference, and you thereby become powerless. If you want to influence a pupil's behaviour, you must avoid educational methods that move the responsibility away from yourself, for example through punishments, consequences, reprimands, or phoning home to the pupil's parents.

5

Children Learn Nothing from Failure

GLORIA

Gloria plays the violin. She has done so since she was seven years old. At the age of ten she plays tolerably. She practises two hours a week and has 25-minute lessons once a week. On Christmas Eve she wants to play Christmas carols at home. Her parents listen patiently. But Gloria is not very good at hitting the right notes, the timing is not quite right, and she doesn't remember everything. Her brother Charlie, who is 12, says: 'No, you've got to stop now. It sounds awful!' Gloria answers: 'But I'm only ten. Of course it's not perfect.'

TO SUCCEED OR NOT TO SUCCEED

This principle builds on research by the Dutch psychologist Anna van Duijvenvoorde and her colleagues. In 2008 they were able to show that children under the age of 15 don't learn anything from finding out that what they are doing is wrong. The research group used magnetic resonance imaging to measure brain activity during various tasks. The experiment was simple: each person was given a number of problems to solve in about 15 minutes, without knowing how they were meant to go about it. If they answered correctly they were rewarded with praise of the type 'That was correct'. If they answered incorrectly on the other hand, they were informed 'That was incorrect'. Van Duijvenvoorde was interested in finding out whether we learn in the same way regardless of whether we learn from success or failure.

The results were totally unexpected. When children in the study over 15 years of age were informed that they had answered incorrectly, brain activity increased in parts of the brain that are involved in learning. If the same children instead were informed that they had answered correctly, brain activity in the same areas fell dramatically. When the same experiment was done with children under the age of 11 the opposite was found. When they found out that they had answered correctly, activity rose, and when they found out they had made a mistake it fell.

In Anna van Duijvenvoorde's opinion, an increase in brain activity is a sign of learning, which means that from the age of 15 you learn from failure, whereas children under the age of 11 learn from success. Between the ages of 11 and 15 it varies a little from child to child. The researchers interpret this as an indication that children of this age develop at different rates, where some learn from success and others from failure. If the children are ordinary children, that is.

The theory on which the study and its conclusions are based says that you learn from happenings that deviate from the normal. Ordinary children are unsuccessful all the time when they are little, but they get better with age, and somewhere around the age of 15 they start to succeed more often than not. Little children are surprised when they succeed, not when they fail. For adults it's the opposite. This is one of the reasons many children stop doing a sport or playing an instrument around the ages of 13 to 15.

They suddenly discover that they are not very good and quit. Only the good ones carry on. As adults, though, we are not surprised when someone tells us we are good. We just don't know how to respond. Perhaps this is a result of the reduced brain activity that Anna van Duijvenvoorde was able to demonstrate.

Children, on the other hand, are not at all surprised when something goes wrong. I remember once around the age of ten when I got home and threw my jacket on the floor as usual. After a while I heard my mum say: 'Bo, how come your jacket's on the floor?' I thought: 'How can she be surprised about that? I always throw my jacket on the floor.' So I replied: 'Because I threw it there.' Unfortunately that wasn't the answer she wanted.

CHILDREN'S AGE AND ABILITIES DETERMINE HOW THEY SHOULD BE APPROACHED

If we are to take Anna van Duijvenvoorde's research seriously, then we should avoid reprimanding children under the age of 15. It probably has no effect anyway. A better idea is to tell them how to succeed better next time instead, and by all means to let them know when they have done well, preferably by praising their efforts: 'You worked so well. And you succeeded, too. Look, it's right!'

Youths over the age of 15 on the other hand can be reprimanded by calmly telling them what went wrong. But only if it is an exception that things go wrong. For youths who are unsuccessful over and over again it has absolutely no effect. Only children and youths who succeed more often than not will have any use of the reprimands they receive. The children you were thinking of when you chose to read this book probably don't fit into that category – they probably belong to the 10 to 15 per cent who far into adult life are still surprised when something goes right.

If these thoughts are applied to teaching in schools it gets even more interesting. We have seen that pupils in primary school learn from succeeding. This means that lots of smileys are effective. Red marks in the maths exercise book, on the other hand, have no effect at all. It's much better to explain how it should be done one more time and then give them new exercises.

Only at the beginning of secondary school can we start pointing out when something has gone wrong, and only for the pupils who manage best with their schoolwork. In the first years of secondary school perhaps most of the pupils will belong to the group that is used to succeeding. But for the two or three pupils in each class who are still unsuccessful much of the time at the end of the ninth year, we primarily need to provide praise in order for them to learn.

CHILDREN LEARN BY SUCCEEDING

Since children under the age of 11 don't learn by failing but by succeeding, this implies that an objection I often hear – 'If we adapt too much then the pupil won't learn anything' – becomes meaningless. If the school has a good educational framework that is adapted to the pupils' varying abilities, then they will succeed and therefore also learn. This means that eventually they will get so used to being successful that they will also start learning from being unsuccessful. And conversely, the more children are unsuccessful during childhood, the less they will learn from this in the long term, and the objection above is therefore incorrect.

All of this can be summarised as follows: children can only learn from a lack of success by first succeeding a great deal.

Summary

Most adults learn something every time they are unsuccessful. That's why we seldom make the same mistake several times. Children on the other hand can be unsuccessful in the same way over and over again without seeing it as a problem. Instead, they learn when they succeed. So don't use methods such as reprimands and punishments when pupils are unsuccessful – rather praise them when they succeed.

6

You Need Self-control to Cooperate with Others

NIDAL

Nidal is described by his parents and teachers as a hot-tempered boy. He easily loses his temper, and on occasion he has got into fights or thrown things at other children when angry. One day, Nidal's classmate Andy walks past his chair during a maths class and whispers: 'Your mother!' Nidal gets up and runs after Andy, who quickly goes out into the corridor, finds a toilet, and locks himself in. Nidal stands and kicks at the door.

The teacher, Camilla, goes out into the corridor and asks Nidal to stop and to come back into the classroom. It *is* maths class, and he's meant to be working. Nidal shouts: 'Shut up, moron.' Camilla chooses to go back into the classroom again. After about ten minutes Nidal follows. Andy is still locked inside the toilet.

After another five minutes Camilla says: 'Start working now, Nidal. We'll talk about it later.' But Nidal can't work. He's restless. The adrenaline is still coursing through his body. He sits mumbling to himself for the rest of the lesson.

Only at the beginning of the next lesson does Andy slip out of the toilet and join the class. By then Camilla has already had time to talk to Nidal and he has calmed down. But he can't work very well during that lesson either. Only after lunch is he sufficiently back in balance to work well.

IT DOESN'T HELP TO REPRIMAND CHILDREN IN AFFECT

The principle 'You must be in control of yourself in order to cooperate with others' is simple. We often think that we can tell children who are stressed and angry what to do and that they will then calm down. But this is not the case. Children in affect can't think as usual; in this state they act on impulse to a greater degree than otherwise. Neither will raising one's voice in such a situation have the desired effect.

If we look at Nidal's situation in the light of the principles described earlier on, we can see that he lacks the ability to control his anger. He does what makes most sense from his agitated perspective – he wants to hit Andy. When Camilla later talks to him in the corridor, the demands made on his capacity for simultaneous action and regulation of affect are too high; he just can't calm down – his adrenaline levels are too high.

THE AFFECT REGULATION MODEL

In school we have to deal with pupils' anger and lack of self-control in many different situations. Sometimes directly, in order to protect another pupil, and sometimes just by waiting and keeping in the background, as in the incident with Nidal.

It is therefore important for us to be aware of what is happening in a situation that we think represents behaviour that challenges, and for us to know how to act in the different phases of such a situation. In 1983, the researchers Stephen Kaplan and Eugenie Wheeler constructed a basic model for an outburst of affect (the assault cycle), which has since appeared in countless different versions. Figure 6.1 shows my version, the affect regulation model.

The strength of the affect is shown on the vertical line and time on the horizontal line. The curve in the model describes the development of affect in a conflict or chaos situation, while the horizontal line in the middle illustrates how much affect a person can handle without starting to fight, bite, throw furniture, scream, or in other ways fall into chaos. Newborn babies can't take very much: they lose control every time they get hungry. So for them, the line in the model is very low. With age, tolerance of affect improves, however, and the line in the model rises. This represents maturing. As adults, we can later handle most situations, and the line will therefore end up above the curve for most of us.

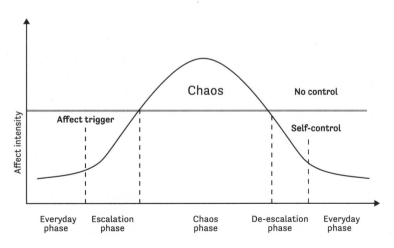

Figure 6.1 The affect regulation model

For pupils with behaviour that challenges at school, though, the line is considerably lower than for most others. This means that they more often than others lose control of themselves, something that can be called inadequate capacity for regulation of affect.

THE MODEL'S DIFFERENT FIELDS

As shown, the model is divided into five fields, which describe five different phases of an outbreak of affect: *everyday calm*, *escalation*, *chaos*, *de-escalation*, and *everyday calm*. In the first phase, the everyday calm phase, the intensity of affect is low. The pupil works on as usual in class or is together with friends. Then comes a trigger factor, an affect trigger. In Nidal's case it was when Andy said: 'Your mother!' The affect trigger leads to the second phase, the escalation phase, taking over. Here it is still possible to communicate with the pupil, but not as well as in the everyday phase. There is still a chance of resolving the situation, however, something the pupils themselves are often interested in doing in this phase. If this is not successful the situation sometimes progresses into the third phase, the chaos phase. Here the pupil is beyond reach and no longer acts strategically. After a while (because it always passes), the pupil gradually calms down, and via the fourth phase, the de-escalation phase, eventually returns to the everyday calm level again, the fifth phase.

All pupils behave differently in the different phases, and different methods are therefore needed in the different phases for the specific situation to be handled in a good way. I will look at this in the coming chapters and also in the second part of the book.

The most important thing for you to take with you from this chapter is the knowledge that it is only possible to cooperate with a pupil who lies below the line in the model. If the pupil's intensity of affect crosses the line, then there is no possibility whatsoever for you to communicate with them. You have the best opportunities for cooperation during the everyday calm phase when the pupil has full self-control. During the escalation and de-escalation phases it is more difficult but still possible. But it will require a much higher degree of adjustment on your part to succeed just then, because in these phases the pupil is fully occupied with trying to maintain control. In the chaos phase, all forms of cooperation are impossible.

Summary
For a pupil to do what you tell them to, they must first have full self-control. To do what someone else tells you is like handing over or lending control to someone else. And to do that you need to have control. Therefore cooperation requires all concerned to be in control of themselves.

7

Everyone Does What They Can to Maintain Self-control

ELAINE

Elaine is having a bad day. The morning was difficult. Her mother woke her up too early, and since then things have gone from bad to worse. She left home without her training clothes and so she had to do PE in her jeans. After PE, her friends, and especially Mary, teased her and said she smelled of sweat. At lunch she finds that they're having fish, which is the last straw. She leaves the canteen and goes in to the toilet. When the lesson is about to start she's still sitting there. The teacher asks where she is, and Mary says she's in the toilet because she smells disgusting. The teacher goes to the toilet and talks to Elaine through the door. Elaine doesn't want to go back to class if stupid Mary is there. After a while the teacher fetches the caretaker who unlocks the door. Elaine tries to hit the teacher, squeezes past her, and runs home.

WE DO ALL WE CAN TO AVOID
LOSING OUR SELF-CONTROL

This principle is simple – we all do what we can to avoid losing control. This isn't so strange. None of us want to throw furniture around, break windows, scream, fight, or bang our head on the wall. So we do what we can so as not to end up in chaos. An effort that is even greater for those in the escalation phase of the model described in the previous chapter.

Some good and effective strategies for maintaining self-control are:

- Try to move away from difficult situations in order to get some peace and quiet.

- Screen yourself off so that you can remain in the situation but the difficult part doesn't feel as difficult.

- Decide that everything is going to be OK and concentrate on this.

- Do something familiar in order to feel more secure.

- Seek support from others, for example members of staff.

In some cases both we and the pupils use other strategies that may be effective but that are probably not well received by those around us; for example:

- Refuse to participate and just say 'no'. This is perhaps the simplest method and also the most dangerous. Very many conflicts between teachers and pupils start with a demand that the pupil refuses.

- Lie in order to manage a difficult situation. The Canadian researcher Victoria Talwar has shown that we lie to protect ourselves if this is the simplest solution. Adults most often do it in a more sophisticated way, so that it's not discovered. Children find lying more difficult, and some children lie so badly that they're discovered at once. To lie well requires that you are good at working out what others are thinking, feeling, and experiencing. Pupils with behaviour that challenges often have not developed this ability as well as others. This means that we have to take this missing competence into account when dealing with pupils who lie a lot. They are doing their best, but their best is not very good.

- Threaten to go away or to hit someone.

- Run away, as George did in the first chapter.

- Try to hit others so that they keep away.

- Seek social affirmation by using insults and the like.

The latter strategies may be experienced as behaviour that challenges. But we must be aware that they are strategies used by the pupil with the intention of resolving a situation, not of making it deteriorate further. This means that we must try to avoid putting a moral filter on such forms of behaviour. They are not wrong in themselves and another alternative would probably be worse. If we want to influence a pupil's behaviour we must go back to the various principles and find out why the behaviour arose. Only by changing the circumstances can we ensure that it will not happen again. It may be as easy as asking the pupil why they acted in a certain way and, based on the reply, discussing with the pupil how to find a better solution next time.

OFFER THE PUPIL AN ALTERNATIVE STRATEGY

By far the worst thing we can do in a difficult situation is to demand that pupils refrain from using a certain strategy without at the same time offering them an alternative. It's quite effective, for example, to talk to the pupils about what they can do next time they end up in a similar situation. To only say 'You mustn't do that. Surely you can see that it turns out wrong' unfortunately does not give the pupil enough support to actually refrain from doing the same thing again. At least not the pupil with a tendency to use the kind of methods you see as behaviour that challenges. This is especially noticeable during the escalation phase (see the model above). Here the ultimate aim, regardless of method, must be for the pupil to maintain full self-control.

Summary
Pupils always do their best to maintain self-control. Much of what you see as behaviour that challenges in fact consists of strategies that the pupil is using to maintain self-control, in order to be able to cooperate. If you counteract the pupil's strategies it will often lead to a worsening of the behaviour that challenges.

8

Affect Is Contagious

THEO

Theo is a restless boy. It's a bit more difficult for him to sit still than for the others in his class. He glides around on his chair when he's supposed to be listening or working at his desk. He's very active during breaks and plays a lot of football.

Theo has two teachers. Pearl is his main teacher and teaches English. Pearl is a dedicated person, on fire for her subject. She loves to get the pupils to discuss texts and what they mean for the pupils' own lives. Pearl finds situations where the pupils don't engage themselves extremely difficult. If a pupil throws a rubber instead of taking part in the discussion, for example, she can get really angry.

One day, late in the afternoon, Theo is quite tender and is having difficulty concentrating in his English class. He starts moving around on his chair and knocks over a book, and with it his papers and pencils. Everything falls on the floor. In the confusion, Theo's chair also tips over, and he falls backwards. Pearl gets angry and shouts: 'Theo! Pick up your things and leave the classroom. Why can you never learn to sit properly like everyone else?' Theo gets angry in turn: 'Why do I have to go? I fell over because your class was so damn boring that I couldn't concentrate!' Then he leaves.

After the lesson Pearl talks about the incident in the staff room. She thinks Theo is a pain in the neck who can never do what he's meant to and is just a disturbance because of his restlessness. She's also tired of him screaming and shouting in class every time she tells him off. Theo's other teacher, Peter, who is a very calm person, says: 'Theo? Sure, he has a little trouble sitting still, but you'd have to look far to find a more polite and hard-working boy.'

AFFECT IS CONTAGIOUS – MIRROR NEURON PROCESSES

The principle 'Affect is contagious' was formulated by the American psychologist Silvan Tomkins in the 1960s. He built his thinking on observations made as early as the 1880s by researchers in psychology. The one who later discovered how it really works was the Italian neurophysiologist Giacomo Rizzolatti at the University of Parma. In the 1990s he discovered that the activity pattern in the brain of a person performing a certain action is mirrored in the brains of others. This means that if someone smiles, then the same activity will be repeated in the brains of those looking at the person, as if they were smiling themselves; this can also make them actually start smiling. In other words, we experience other people's feelings by being infected with them ourselves. It is easier to be happy if you are together with happy people, and it has a calming effect to be with calm people. In the same way, it is easier to get angry at an angry person – someone who shouts and screams has a tendency to make other people shout and scream.

The extent to which people can screen out other people's feelings varies. Most pupils (and teachers) are only affected to a limited degree by how others around them feel, some are affected very little by others' feelings, and still others are completely dominated by other people's feelings. In an ordinary class you will probably find all kinds, which means that the pupils and the mood in the class will be affected by the teacher's mood, or by a pupil who is restless.

Theo is sensitive to other people's feelings. His ability to concentrate is affected by how much fuss other people make, so Pearl and Theo make a bad combination. Pearl's dedication and extrovert personality affect Theo so much that it reduces his ability to manage at school. Pearl's temper is the biggest problem; when she gets angry Theo reacts strongly. He is influenced a lot by other people's affect and can't regulate his own affect as well as other people. This means that he feels good and develops well when he has calm teachers around him who are good at controlling their affect, but gets stressed by Pearl's energy and temperament.

THE LOW-AROUSAL APPROACH

If we go back to the principles from the earlier chapters, we can conclude that Pearl is placing demands that are too high on Theo's ability to regulate his affect. Since she is the teacher and he is the pupil, she is the one who needs to change her ways. Alternatively, in order to take responsibility for his learning, she can shield Theo by letting him work more on his own.

Problems of this type increase in importance the more conflicts we have with a pupil. I often find that the more conflicts you have, the more decided the tone of voice and body language become. If, in demand situations, we use marked body language, demand eye contact, or move closer to the pupil, the affect will just be more infectious, which will result in the pupil also becoming more determined and the risk of conflict increasing. To reduce the risk of conflict, the following are important:

- *Never demand eye contact.* This is a simple dominance tool, which most often results in escalation of a conflict.

- *Never maintain eye contact for more than three seconds in a demand or conflict situation.* Eye contact for more than three seconds leads to a powerful transmission of affect in either a positive or negative direction, but never in the direction the school wants. The American psychiatrist and development psychologist Daniel Stern once said that 30 seconds of eye contact ends in either violence or sex.

- *Take a step back in demand situations and situations of potential conflict.* By moving closer to the pupil when you make demands or mark a limit, you are increasing the pupil's stress level. If you instead take a step back at the same time as you make a demand, the stress from the demand will be balanced by the reduced transmission of affect.

- *Sit down if the pupil is uneasy.* Or lean against a wall. A relaxed body is as contagious as a tense body, and you want the pupil to be relaxed.

- *Distract instead of confronting.* By shifting the pupil's focus you prevent the transmission of affect that arises between you and the pupil in situations where you want to mark a limit. You distract by making the pupil think about something else. During the

DISRUPTIVE, STUBBORN, OUT OF CONTROL?

escalation phase mentioned in the model described in Chapter 6, distraction is perhaps the most important active intervention there is.

- *Don't take hold of a pupil with tensed muscles.* Muscle tension is just as contagious as affect. If you have to take hold of a pupil, do it gently and move with the pupil's movements. To physically restrain a pupil by holding them tight will in most cases lead to violent conflict.

THE ONE WHO WINS LOSES

There is a minor principle which perhaps deserves a chapter of its own and which I will return to in Chapter 11 on leadership in the classroom – namely, 'The one who wins loses.' By this I mean that if we win a conflict with a pupil, it will not improve the pupil's learning or cooperation, since it will negatively affect the alliance between pupil and teacher. On the other hand, if the pupil wins a conflict, they will fail to learn whatever it was we were trying to teach them by holding on to our demand. Since we don't want the pupil to lose, neither of us can be allowed to win. Methods that are based on dominance do not belong in today's school. We must get the pupils to move in the same direction as us, rather than creating a relationship of opposition.

Summary

We are all influenced by one another's feelings. If we are together with happy people we become happy; and similarly, angry people make us angry. Pupils with behaviour that challenges are often more highly influenced than others by the affect of those around them. It is therefore important that you are not confrontational and angry in the way you express yourself, since it will rub off on the pupil. By moderating your body language and tone of voice, you can reduce the number of conflicts with pupils.

9

Conflicts Consist of Solutions and Failures Require an Action Plan

VICTOR

Victor and his class are having a swimming lesson. They are meant to be swimming 200 metres. There are 15 children in the pool but only five lanes to swim in. Victor swims a little slower than most of his classmates. After a while Nicholas catches up and tries to swim past him. Victor doesn't like losing competitions and it's hard for him to accept being overtaken in the swimming pool. And on top of everything, Nicholas catches him with a kick when he's almost past. Victor gets angry. He grabs Nicholas' leg and pulls him back. Nicholas splashes wildly, thinking he's about to drown.

The swimming instructor, Stephen, goes between the boys and holds them apart, saying, 'Calm down now. Nicholas, you swim ahead; Victor, you wait here for a bit.' Victor isn't very happy with this solution. He tries to get past Stephen, but Stephen blocks the lane effectively. So Victor swims over to the side instead, and stays there, sulking. Stephen is upset that Victor won't do what he's told and swims up to him underwater, appearing behind him, and says: 'You must do as I tell you. If you don't swim your 200 metres then you won't meet the requirements. Now back into your lane again!'

Victor, who still hasn't calmed down, answers: 'Watch it. I'm not swimming any more with idiots like you in the pool. You grabbed me, you devil. That is damn well not OK.' Stephen gets angry: 'If you don't want to swim then get out of the pool. Go shower and get dressed.' But Victor doesn't intend to leave the pool; instead he splashes water at Stephen and says: 'Just leave me alone.' Stephen grabs Victor, lifts him out of the water and partly up on the edge of the pool, and tries to get out himself. Victor gets up and pushes Stephen down into the water with his foot. Stephen swims over to the ladder, gets out, and says: 'Off to the changing room with you. That's quite enough!' Victor tries to push Stephen into the pool again, so then Stephen picks him up and carries him out to the changing room. Victor hits, kicks, and screams, but takes his clothes and goes home when Stephen lets go of him.

ASHTON

Ashton and Mohammad have had PE. They have been playing football, and adrenaline levels are still a little high. They are late for lunch, and when they get to the canteen there is a queue. They start bickering about who should be first in line.

When it's time to take their trays there's a bit of a row, and Ashton tries to go past Mohammad. Peggy, a teacher who is there with her own class, intervenes: 'Boys, calm down. Go to the back of the line and show me that you know how to stand in line better than that.' Ashton says: 'What do you mean, back of the line? I'm damn well not going to the back of the line just because a stupid teacher tells me to.' But Peggy doesn't relent: 'You will do as I say. Go to the back of the line, now!'

Ashton and Mohammad stay in the line but keep quiet. Ashton takes a plate and starts putting spaghetti on it.

Then Peggy takes him by the arm: 'Put the plate down and leave. You can't carry on like this, there's no lunch for you today.' Ashton twists free of her grip and ignores her.

Carl, another teacher, sees what's happening and decides to get involved. He goes up to Ashton, picks him up, and carries him out of the dining room. On the way, Ashton screams insults, tries to hit Carl, and tries to wriggle loose. When Carl puts him down, Ashton kicks him on the shins and runs away down the corridor, banging on the windows as he goes.

CONFLICTS CONSIST OF SOLUTIONS

In this chapter two principles will be discussed, firstly the principle that 'Conflicts consist of solutions' and then the principle 'Failures require an action plan', which will be referred to a little further on.

The principle 'Conflicts consist of solutions' is simple. If we examine each person's actions step by step in the stories above, we see that the situations develop according to a simple pattern. One person runs into a problem. The person solves the problem, usually in a way that causes a problem for someone else. This person then uses a solution that in turn becomes a problem for the first person, who needs to find a solution in the next step. And most likely this solution will also lead to a problem for the other person. A situation can thus progress through a series of solutions where each solution is a problem for the other party. The level of violence increases with each solution, until finally physical conflict ensues.

This type of conflict can only be resolved by one party finding a solution that is not a problem for the other party. And this is where it gets interesting. Because in most cases that I have encountered in my work I have been called in to answer the question of how the school can get the pupil to find a solution that is not a problem for the teachers. Instead of thinking the other way around.

WHEN WE ADULTS THINK WE HAVE TO WIN

In school, you as a teacher are the professional. You are the one with the responsibility for everyday school life and for the pupils' well-being, development, and learning. How in the world then can the school arrive at the idea that the teacher's problems in the classroom and the schoolyard should be solved by the pupils? It seems much more reasonable and straightforward that you as a teacher should find a solution that is not a problem for the pupils.

In both of the situations above, the teachers working with Victor and Ashton think they must win. They think they can domineer their way through the situations and that Victor and Ashton are the ones who need to change their behaviour. This attitude has the effect that Peggy, Carl, and Stephen deprive themselves of the possibility to make a difference, since, after all, they don't succeed in their actions. To use methods like those used by Peggy, Carl, and Stephen in the situations with Victor and Ashton carries a serious risk of failure. It is therefore necessary to find solutions with less risk.

A good way of handling this situation is based on not creating problems for the pupil. In the first situation, Victor actually uses a solution that should not be a problem for Stephen. To calm down at the side of the pool, for example, is a good strategy on his part. The problem is that Stephen thinks he must win the fight with Victor; that's what makes things spiral out of control. Stephen simply doesn't want to be the one to lose.

In the second situation, Peggy makes a demand, which implies that she wins and Ashton loses if he does as she says.

He doesn't want to lose. But because Peggy has made such a clear demand, one of them is going to lose. In reality, everyone loses when any of those involved in a situation think they have won. Stephen is going to find it difficult to teach Victor effectively after a conflict like this. And it will be difficult for both Peggy and Carl to achieve the authority needed for Ashton to do what they tell him next time they happen to meet.

FAILURES REQUIRE AN ACTION PLAN

In order to make any progress after suffering a defeat in school, you need to follow the principle 'Failures require an action plan'. The principle was formulated in the aftermath of the death of Matthew Goodman. Matthew was a 14-year-old boy with significant special needs. He went to a training school and died because he couldn't breathe after a fall. The fall was due to his arms and legs being mechanically immobilised with splints. The court considered it a failure that the school was unable to help a pupil using methods based on educational science, and instead limited the pupil's freedom of movement. In this case the failing resulted in Matthew's death and in the formulation of *Matthew's Law*, which in essence says that all restraints are a failure and all failures require an action plan.

When you are about to make an action plan you can start by evaluating the failure using the affect regulation model (see Chapter 6). In the case of Victor's and Ashton's conflicts with Stephen, Peggy, and Carl, it's easy to find the trigger factors, namely the clear demands made in the form of reprimands. It is also fairly easy to conclude that the methods they all use in the escalation phase don't have the desired effect, that is – that the pupils will regain their self-control. Neither are the methods that they resort to in the next phase, the chaos phase, very good. They don't lead to any improvement in Victor's and Ashton's situation.

AVOID PHYSICAL RESTRAINT

Specifically in the chaos phase, it is important not to restrain the pupil's freedom of movement. If we carry away or restrain a pupil, the chaos phase will increase dramatically in length. If the pupil furthermore is restrained with tensed muscles, this will increase the pupil's muscle tension in turn, and thereby their stress, adrenaline flow, and risk of becoming violent. The most effective thing to do is most often to try to move other pupils away rather than trying to move the pupil with the outburst of affect. If absolutely necessary, we can separate pupils who are fighting in order to avoid immediate serious danger to life and health. This can pass as an emergency and could therefore be considered acceptable.

To resort to actions only permissible in emergencies is by definition something that as a teacher you only do when there is an emergency – that is, in rare and unpredictable situations. I have sometimes met teachers who told me they had restrained a pupil at regular intervals when they had had outbursts. This can never be considered an emergency. If a pupil is violent at regular intervals it is not unpredictable. If this happens we need to find out what demands and expectations the school has in such situations, so that they can be avoided.

RESTRAINING SOMEONE THREE TIMES IS A METHOD – AND NO LONGER AN EMERGENCY

So it is possible to resort to actions permissible only in emergencies once or twice when a new situation arises.

But the third time it happens it has become a method. Which means that the concept of emergency is no longer applicable. Stephen above, for example, is not allowed to make a method of carrying out pupils who don't want to swim, and Carl can't make a method of carrying out pupils who make a fuss in the canteen. They must instead change the circumstances so that this type of incident does not happen again. Their failures demand that the school make an action plan for this kind of situation. I will touch on this again, later in the book.

Summary

Most conflicts consist of a series of solutions, where each party in turn tries to solve the problems that the other person's solutions have created for them. This type of situation can only be resolved by one party finding a solution that is not a problem for the other party. It is therefore important for the school to find a way to solve the problem, a way that does not cause a problem for the pupil and so prevents conflicts from escalating.

10

Teaching Is Making Demands that the Pupils Would Not Have Made on Themselves — In a Way that Works

LEIA

Leia thinks that maths is so-so. Quite fun when she can do it, especially when the questions are in colour. One day the teacher comes into class and says: 'Now it's maths. Today we are going to learn how to divide.' Leia hasn't a clue what division is. If she hadn't gone to school she probably wouldn't have learnt how to divide. The thought would probably never have crossed her mind that it might be something useful for her to know.

SORAN

Soran goes to kindergarten. After eating, the teacher says: 'Come, let's go out in the hall and put our shoes and overalls on. We're going out to play!' If she hadn't said this, Soran would probably have walked around aimlessly, looking at what the others were doing and maybe pushing someone so that at least something happened.

LIZZIE

Lizzie is angry at Megan. Megan has taken Lizzie's pencil case and poured out the contents on the floor, and now she's teasing Lizzie about her My Little Pony rubber. So Lizzie has grabbed hold of Megan's hair. Their teacher, Laurie, says: 'Stop it now, girls. Come, let's pick up the pencils and rubbers.'

WHEN EVERYDAY DEMANDS BECOME A PROBLEM

The first part of the principle 'Teaching is making demands that the pupils would not have made on themselves' is easy to relate to. If it wasn't true, we wouldn't have needed any school, any teachers, or any education. All teaching is about getting pupils to do things they wouldn't have done if it hadn't been in the school context. The demands that the school is permitted to make are sometimes regulated by law and curriculum. Those demands are not a problem. The problems arise when you start to make demands that are not described in the curriculum or the law but are considered part of everyday teaching, as you undoubtedly already do, or will do. It may be asking the pupils to take out their books, put on their shoes, eat politely, or stop calling each other names.

TAKING AWAY THE PUPILS' AUTONOMY

The American philosopher Martha Nussbaum proposes that teachers and care staff to some extent take away the basic right of autonomy. This is an interesting perspective. And I definitely see where she's coming from. Of course the school can't let the children themselves decide what they want to do and how they are going to learn. As a teacher, you obviously want to decide on the programme for the day, set up rules, and be able to demand a certain standard of behaviour from your pupils, something that implies a fairly big responsibility for both you and everybody else working in schools. Nussbaum says that the fact that the school takes away the pupils' autonomy does not really need to be a problem in itself, but that there always must be a good argument for doing so. Always.

The arguments that I think are relevant when it comes to the possibility of taking away the pupils' autonomy are:

- *Avoidance of danger.* Pupils in kindergarten and primary school should be in school. They should not have the freedom that older pupils have to go to the shop outside the school at breaks. This is not very controversial. It is more controversial that children in kindergarten often have no possibility at all to get out of the kindergarten because the handles are placed too high for them to reach. In most of the world the basic principle is that you are not allowed to lock people up without some kind of court order giving you that right, either from the criminal courts or via special laws on psychiatric care. But it is understandable to place the handles high up in order to avoid danger. This is also the argument for taking actions only permissible in emergencies, such as holding on to pupils to stop them running out into the traffic.

- *Care.* It is easy to use the care argument when demanding good hygiene, for example. To avoid danger, one can use quite far-reaching methods, bordering on domination and force. This is not possible with the care argument. Taking hold of a child on their way out into the traffic would not be seen as excessive, but forcibly brushing the teeth of a fourth-year pupil would, in many people's view, definitely be crossing the line. One can use various tricks and even some manipulative tools when resorting to the care argument. For example, one can permit oneself to put swimming on a pupil's schedule to ensure that they shower at least once a week.

- *Increasing real autonomy.* This is the most powerful argument. Many pupils can't handle full autonomy, but on the other hand probably not all adults can either. Society has decided to limit citizens' autonomy on certain points. Traffic is a good example. Parliaments all over the world have decided that you are only allowed to drive on one side of the road. This is an enormous limitation of ordinary people's autonomy and right to decide for themselves, but at the same time it entails a dramatic increase in autonomy relating to where you want to go. If you could drive on either side of the road, you wouldn't get very far. The school curriculum is based on similar arguments. By deciding what pupils should learn in primary school, it broadens the possibilities they have in choosing a career.

The last argument is also possible to apply in situations such as breaks and other spare time. Some pupils are very good at structuring their time and finding good things to do, and they very seldom end up in conflicts. Other children don't have these abilities. For these, it is a good thing if someone else structures break activities for them, either via agreement or suggestion. They may even need several suggestions to choose from in order to get a feeling of autonomy. Otherwise they may just go out at breaks, look for where something fun is happening, and go there. This does not reflect real autonomy, but rather just impulse-driven behaviour. So however strange it may sound, by limiting the possible choices for its pupils, the school can actually increase their real autonomy.

THE CRAFT OF TEACHING

One of the principles we have already covered is that 'people do what makes sense' (see Chapter 3). This implies that if the school chooses to direct a pupil's behaviour in a certain direction (because there are good arguments for doing so), then making sense can work as an aid. One could say that making sense is the best tool to achieve the final part of this chapter's principle, 'making demands in a way that works'. All crafts have their tools, and making sense is one of the foremost tools of the teaching craft.

There are different ways to improve the sense of appropriate behaviour. The simplest is for the school to offer the pupils structures that make sense, something I have touched on already concerning physical structures, rules, and time-related structures for creating predictability.

Structures that make sense are quite simply the foundation of good teaching. If the school can offer this, if the physical framework provides the scope and necessary conditions for good behaviour, and if you and your colleagues can lay the foundation for a predictable school day for the pupils – then the school has come far. But you must also make activities seen as incomprehensible by the pupils make sense, regardless of what you are trying to do. If the activities are important, then you must find ways of making them make sense to the pupils. This is what the teaching craft is all about.

MAKING ACTIVITIES MAKE SENSE

Incomprehensible activities can be made to make sense for the pupils in different ways:

- *Increase the feeling of participation.* If the pupils feel they have all taken part in deciding to do an activity then it is easier to get them to cooperate. This does not mean that they have to decide on the activities at a high, overall level. Sometimes participation in the little things is enough. You can say, for example: 'Here is a sheet with ten maths problems. You must do at least four, but you can decide which ones to do.' Strangely enough, this works better than just giving them four problems.

- *Create a feeling of belonging.* If a pupil feels noticed by you, this increases confidence and trust. If the pupil has confidence in you, this is often enough to create understandability around following instructions and living up to expectations. It implies, however, that you must make sure the demands you make are not too high for the pupil, otherwise confidence will decrease and behaviour that challenges will increase. A classic trick in kindergarten is to say: 'Come, let's go get ourselves a clean nappy.' You can also try to create a feeling of belonging and participation by letting the pupils do things together; the experience of belonging and participation with friends can be effective in increasing understandability. It requires, however, that at least one pupil can act as a motor.

- *Prepare the pupils for what is coming.* The better prepared the pupils are, the fewer conflicts will arise. It is therefore important to work with timetables, both traditional school timetables as well as schedules for the content and flow of lessons, break activities, and perhaps most important of all, for what is going to happen in the typically less-structured subjects such as art, crafts, and physical education. It can also be a matter of preparing to round off an activity by announcing when there's five minutes left. One little exception: the only situation where a fixed time warning (such as five minutes) is not effective is when you are going to interrupt an activity that would be more natural to stop at a later point. In this case a time warning is a blunt tool, which may even increase the level of conflict. You can't prepare someone to leave a cinema in the middle of a film by saying: 'We're leaving in five minutes.' In the same way, some pupils can't stop playing on the computer in the middle of a game just because the break is over, even if they have been warned in advance.

- *Increase sense through out-and-out tricks.* An example of this is that you get an activity going with a prompt, for example you take out their books for pupils who have a hard time getting them out of their bags. They will most likely start working when the books are lying right in front of them. It will simply be hard not to start working when they are lying there. Just as most kids do take a shower if you hand them a towel and ask them to.

- *Finished is another trick.* When pupils have just finished doing something, it is often easy for them to immediately start doing something else. Some activities have a clear 'finish', such as eating, watching a film, or playing a level in a computer game. When you want to prepare a pupil for a new activity you can say: 'When you are finished with that level we will...' Then most people can stop and do something else. Finished also works in group situations. If, for example, you are on a school trip and you want the children to be ready to go back to school at the same time, you can offer them an ice cream or a banana. Everyone then stops what they are doing in order to eat, and when the ice cream or banana is finished everyone is ready to go home.

- *Add motivating features.* You can do this by making a competition out of a boring assignment or adding fun to situations which you know could become chaotic. It's simply a matter of making the assignment more exciting by adding something that is interesting or fun to do. This is the same factor that makes it easier to read a book with a little colour than one that is just black and white.

DISTRACTION IS BETTER THAN SETTING LIMITS

One of the most difficult situations at school is setting limits. If a pupil is behaving in a way that needs to be interrupted, then the demand made is often very clear and reproving of the pupil. There is unfortunately no evidence to show that setting limits leads to a change in behaviour in the long term, however. At best, your action constitutes management of an acute situation, but such management is risky.

Norwegian research by the psychologist Stål Bjørkly has shown that violence against members of staff often starts in limit-setting situations. If a pupil is felt to be disruptive, it easily happens that they are reprimanded. This will not lead to a change in the long term, however, but rather increases the risk that the situation will end in conflict. In this situation, distraction is a better alternative. By starting to talk about things that interest the pupil, for example catching their attention or just getting them to think about something else, you can make the pupil stop the disruptive behaviour. Not all pupils need to be distracted, of course, but for the few who respond well, you can dramatically reduce conflicts by using distraction in your way of working (see Chapter 13 for more examples of distraction).

Summary

Teaching often implies that you make demands of your pupils that they would not make of themselves. This is meaningless, however, if the pupils are unable to live up to the demands. Good teaching practice is therefore to make relevant demands of the pupils in a way that enables them to live up to the demands. It is thus important how you make your demands, something that could be called the craft of teaching.

11

You Become a Leader When Someone Follows You

KEVIN

Kevin is having an English class. He thinks English is boring. When his teacher, Martin, starts talking about folksongs, Kevin shows quite plainly that he is not intending to participate. He yawns, sighs, and moves around on his chair.

Martin gets noticeably irritated and tells Kevin to sit still. Kevin answers: 'It's so damn boring. Why do I need to know this stuff? Who the hell needs to know anything about folksongs?' Martin says: 'If you don't want to participate then you can go and explain why to the principal. Go on, off you go.' Kevin refuses and says: 'What for? Why do I have to go to the principal just because I think this is boring?' Martin takes hold of Kevin's arm and pulls him away, out of the classroom. Kevin tears free in the corridor and shouts: 'Fucking pig! I'm going to report you!'

BEING ALLOWED TO LEAD

The principle 'You become a leader when someone follows you' is in one way quite obvious, but at the same time very difficult to understand. Often we think that leading and being in charge are the same thing, and that a good leader should be authoritarian. But this is not so. Leading is not the same thing as being in charge formally – it's about getting other people to let you call the tune. That's why this principle is very much about confidence and trust, but also, on the craftsmanship level, about needing good tools that ensure you will be allowed to lead. In other words, you need tools that help the pupils follow your instructions.

IT IS DIFFICULT TO LEAD

In the summer of 2012, Local Government Denmark (the interest group and member authority of Danish municipalities) sounded an alarm. For several years they had been sending all newly educated teachers on a three-month course in classroom leadership, since they felt that the new teachers lacked knowledge and training in this. In the group's opinion, this was really the teaching colleges' responsibility.

It is difficult to lead. In addition, available research has focused mainly on corporate leadership, which for obvious reasons is something completely different from leading a class of pupils in a learning situation. But there are perhaps still some things to be learnt from what others have thought about leadership, such as the British seventeenth-century philosopher Hobbes, for example. He advocated a form of government that we today would call a dictatorship. He proposed that people give up their freedom to a leader in return for security, rights, and care. If the leader was unable to fulfil the people's needs in these areas then they could take back their freedom. We have seen many examples of this in recent years, not least in the disintegration of Eastern Europe around 1990 and the Arab Spring starting in 2010. The same thing happens of course in democratic countries, but there it most often takes place through elections, according to normal democratic custom.

THE TEACHERS' AUTHORITY

In principle, the contract that Hobbes described also could apply to school. The pupils give up their autonomy in exchange for well-being and education. If the school does not succeed on these points, then the pupils take back full autonomy, either by starting to question the authority or by not appearing. A few decades ago, a teacher could manage fairly well with an authoritarian leadership style, since the pupils were used to that style at home. Today that doesn't work any more. The pupils are used to being listened to; they are used to participating in and influencing all kinds of family decisions, from what they are having for supper to what car the family should buy.

One could of course discuss whether this is good or bad, but we still have to relate to the fact that the situation is as it is. What it means is that you need to have a leadership style that makes the pupils feel included and listened to, in order to be able to establish and maintain any kind of authority. But without being too soft or over-friendly.

AUTHORITY THROUGH UNDERSTANDING THE NATURE OF POWER

Authority is an interesting concept to discuss, but to create and maintain authority you first need to understand the nature of power. Martin, the teacher in the situation above, does not succeed in either creating or maintaining authority by being authoritarian. If we go back a little to a principle previously described, 'The one who wins loses' (see Chapter 8), then we can conclude that Martin both wins and loses the conflict. He wins on one level but loses on two. Partly by not increasing the chances that Kevin will learn anything. And partly because he doesn't succeed in inspiring in Kevin the confidence needed for Kevin to participate in class in a good way next time.

WE MUST DESERVE POWER

Modern society has various forms of authorities. At the top we have the legislative power – that is, the parliament and government. We also have the judicial power in the courts, which uphold the law; and the executive power in the form of the police, who have a monopoly on force – that is, they are the only ones permitted to use force in their exercise of power.

If we extrapolate this to schools, we see that these three forms of power don't exist there. Admittedly the principal stakes out a direction for the school, just like the parliament and government, and in your role as a teacher you sometimes have an executive role reminiscent of that of the police. But neither you nor the principal have the right to use the forms of power that the legislative and executive authorities do. The principal is not allowed to create rules that go beyond the law; and as a teacher, you are not allowed to use force. This means that both the principal and teachers must show themselves deserving of power. Because nowhere in the school's commission does it say that the pupils must do what the teacher tells them to. Yet you still have to ensure that the pupils learn what they should. In other words, you have full responsibility for leading the pupils, but to succeed in doing so you must show that you deserve your authority over them.

CREATE UNDERSTANDABILITY, TRUST, AND INVOLVEMENT

The discussion above leads us back to the concept of understandability discussed earlier (see Chapter 10) – that is, that the pupils do what is most understandable in each situation. It means that we need to create understandability through trust and involvement. We need to make the behaviour that we want from our pupils to be the most understandable behaviour for the pupils themselves in each situation. As touched on earlier, this is partly about us creating structures that make sense via the school's physical framework, rules, and activities. But also about creating confidence in ourselves, and a feeling of involvement in the pupils.

FREEDOM OF SPEECH IN SOCIETY AS A WHOLE

In democracies, the authority of the parliament and government is tied to freedom of speech. This means that people can think what they like about both parliament and government. They can even say it out loud and write it in the papers. If, for example, you think that the government consists of a bunch of unintelligent bunglers then you can write a debate article or send a letter to a paper and argue your case. Or even just say that that's what you think. You don't actually need to say why. Let us suppose for a moment that someone writes a letter to a paper with the following content:

> Now the government has done it again. Without the slightest thought for the nation's well-being, they have approved a budget that means children won't learn what they should, the sick will not get the care they

need, and vulnerable families will be left to fend for themselves in the best way they can. Such an insensitive government has not been seen in this country in the past 100 years. And neither does it mean that taxes will be reduced. No, both bad and expensive! Enough! Out with these unintelligent bunglers and in with those who have a bit of compassion, and an awareness of the consequences of the decisions they are making on our behalf!

This would be a completely legal letter which in most countries would not have entailed any problems whatsoever for the person writing it. Let's now continue the experiment and suppose that the next day there was a letter in the paper from the prime minister, that read as follows:

Yesterday there was a letter in this paper that described me and my colleagues in the government as unintelligent bunglers. I do not consider it acceptable to write in this way. The person who wrote this has no insight into our talents, and seems, to say the least, unintelligent in turn. We in the government are doing a great job for the people, and I think we deserve more respect!

This would also be a legal letter to write. But it would not be received as well as the first. The reason is that we are actually allowed to call the prime minister an unintelligent bungler. You have to be able to take this kind of flak if you are in power. But it is not acceptable for a prime minister to call a critic unintelligent. As a citizen, you are at the mercy of the power behind the prime minister. This means that the prime minister has great responsibility for ensuring that the citizens maintain their confidence in that power.

The prime minister's supposed letter would not promote either confidence or authority; on the contrary, it would undermine the prime minister's authority, not only over the one who wrote the first letter but also among those who read the reply.

THE PUPILS' FREEDOM OF SPEECH

In school, the pupils are at the mercy of our power in the same way that everyone in society is at the mercy of the government. The difference is that the pupils can't vote us out of power in the same way that we can vote the government out of power. This means that the school has a special responsibility when it comes to maintaining authority and leadership.

The letter above could be compared with Kevin's comments at the beginning of the chapter. He ended up calling the teacher a fucking pig. Is this OK? Yes, interesting question.

Calling people names is not uncommon. It is often done between two people with the aim of evening out a perceived inequality. If the individuals are on an equal standing and the one suddenly starts being bossy, it is not unusual for the other to call the first by unflattering names. He may say: 'Who are you to suddenly be in charge? Damn idiot!' And the other may reply in either of two ways:

- 'I'm sorry. We are equal. I shouldn't decide for both of us.' Equality is restored.

- 'What? Damn idiot yourself!' Again equality is restored. Two damn idiots.

Is it OK to call people names in such a situation? Maybe. We do it anyway. Calling people names is a way to try and even out a power relationship.

It gets even more interesting when you go beyond the situation of equality and into the world of the school. For pupils and teachers are not on equal terms.

THE RIGHT TO CRITICISE AUTHORITY

In answer to the question above as to whether it is OK for Kevin to call Martin a fucking pig, my answer would have to be: 'Actually, yes.' Since Martin is the one in power, Kevin can say basically anything he wants to, within the limitations of the law. What is more interesting is to look at the reply alternatives for Martin. If he thought that he and Kevin were on equal terms he could have said: 'Fucking pig yourself!' That would not be an acceptable answer from a teacher to a pupil. But he could also say: 'Don't call me names. It's not OK.' With such an answer he would lose authority, not only in Kevin's eyes but also in the eyes of the other pupils. The answer implies equality, which undermines authority. The name-calling would also increase, since the first occasion had the intended effect, which was to demonstrate that Kevin and Martin are actually equals and that Martin can't decide over Kevin. If he was aware of the relative power balance, on the other hand, he could instead have said: 'So you might think. But you're still going to the principal.' With an answer like this, Martin might have been able to save a little of whatever authority he had, and perhaps the name-calling would have decreased. Unfortunately, in the specific example, Martin renounces his authority by not securing Kevin's confidence in him. He also undermines his own authority by sending Kevin to the principal, which

Kevin can only see as an indication that Martin is unable to handle authority on his own, without help from management.

I sometimes meet teachers who have immense difficulty in seeing authority in this way. They use arguments such as: 'If Kevin is allowed to speak like this then the other pupils will start speaking in the same way. Soon you'll hear the pupils saying anything.' This is not true in my experience. In practice, the great majority of the other pupils won't call their teacher a fucking pig just because Kevin did, in the same way that most of us won't call the government unintelligent bunglers just because someone did in a letter to the paper. Most pupils like their school and want good relationships with their teachers. Kids do well if they can.

The few who don't succeed in this need a greater and different investment from the school. The school's responsibility is then to create a mental environment where the pupils' confidence and feeling of security are so good that there is no invitation to call the teachers names. This also increases the chances that the pupils will meet the learning goals, which is the school's most important assignment. Martin's behaviour in the story above undermines Kevin's chances of achieving these goals, and is therefore an example of poor teaching craftsmanship.

LEADERSHIP IN THE CLASSROOM

There are several aspects of how leadership in the classroom should work that I could mention here. Many I have already discussed in previous chapters, but since a little repetition does no harm, here are a few suggestions for how to get your pupils to do what you tell them to:

- Make sure that the pupils' assignments are interesting, understandable, and meaningful.

- Make sure that the physical framework is optimal with regard to space, sound environment, behaviour-regulating furnishings, and other factors.

- Work actively to get a good relationship with your pupils so that you deserve authority. Joke with them, comfort when necessary, and be aware of their wider life, such as what brothers and sisters they have, hobbies, and the like.

- Create calm in the classroom by investing in:

  ▸ structure and predictability, lists, or schedules for what is going to happen, both in lessons and during breaks

  ▸ understandable rules that the pupils willingly follow because they make sense to them

  ▸ being calm yourself

  ▸ not escalating conflicts by reacting harshly – rather striving for cooperation.

- Maintain authority by not taking it for granted or misusing it.

- Avoid punishments, scolding, and reprimands.

- Make sure the pupils feel fairly treated.

Remember that the one who wins loses, and that you don't become a leader until someone follows you!

Summary

Getting the pupils to learn what they should is easier if they do what you tell them to. But to get them to do what you tell them is not something you learn at college. It depends on how you handle your authority, which is actually something the pupils give you. It's important for you to make it easy for them to do so. Leadership is about getting the pupils to follow you.

Part 2

Cases and Action Plans

12

It's the School's Responsibility to Ensure that the Pupils Achieve the Learning Goals

We have now reached the second part of the book. It discusses how to implement in practice the principle of responsibility (the one who takes responsibility can make a difference) in schools, where to find the tools needed for the task, and last but not least, when to make use of the different tools. Because it is the school's responsibility to carry out the commission it has received from society. And there are no good excuses if the school fails.

We will use sample cases to look more closely at three different scenarios and try to understand them based on the principles in the first part of the book. We will then analyse the situations with the help of the affect regulation model (see Chapter 6) and create relevant action plans for them.

But first of all, here is a useful metaphor which likens school to a car garage intended to carry out the tasks that society has assigned to it.

SCHOOL AS A GARAGE

When my car breaks down I usually take it to the garage. Put simply, I make a contract with the mechanic to do a job that I will pay for. Each of us, car owner and mechanic, expects the other to fulfil their part of the deal. The contract primarily defines who is responsible for what, and the consequences if either party does not live up to its responsibilities.

Society could be seen as having entered into a similar contract with the school. The school should ensure that the pupils reach the learning goals, enable them to progress through the educational system, and, in the long run, to participate in society in various ways. So society (the government and the parents) is the customer, the teacher is the mechanic, and the pupil is the car.

THE MECHANIC'S EXCUSES

Let's suppose that I have left my car at the garage because the engine overheats. The mechanic takes a look and calls me up to say that the water pump is too small and has to be upgraded to one with better performance. I get a fixed price for the job, a bit expensive, but what can you do? After a couple of days I go to the garage to get my car. The mechanic gets paid. Then the problems start. The mechanic says: 'I have done what I could, but I'm afraid the car doesn't work. The engine overheats.' 'What?' I say. 'That's what you were meant to fix!'

The mechanic may then have various different reasons for not having succeeded:

- 'The car wouldn't cooperate during the repairs. It held on to the bolts so that I couldn't get them loose.

I simply had to leave the old water pump where it was. If the car won't cooperate I can't do my job.'

- 'I told the car to turn down the temperature. After all, most cars don't overheat. I think it's a matter of motivation. It can if it wants to.'

- 'When I look at your car I can see that you are a rough driver. No wonder the car overheats. But if you want to drive like you do, it can't be my responsibility to upgrade your water pump. Drive more carefully and everything will work fine. But I still want to get paid, you got great advice here.'

- 'I discovered that the water pump was too small. Things are as they are. There's nothing I can do about it. At my garage we only take care of cars that work. I changed the oil and air filters and checked that all the lamps work. But cars with inefficient water pumps can't be my responsibility. So you can take it home again. The bill is for taking care of your car for several days.'

- 'Unfortunately I don't have the tools needed to change the water pump. Your car is an old American car. The water pump bolts are 1/2 inch bolts. A few years ago we threw out all our inch spanners because new research has shown that metric spanners are more effective, now that most cars are imported. In this garage we only use evidence-based methods and nowadays there are significantly better results with metric spanners. I did try with a 13-millimetre spanner, but it slipped, so unfortunately now the bolt heads are ruined. The car is actually in worse shape than when you left it. But I did my best! And I spent lots of time on it, which of course I want to be paid for. What's worse, I ruined my knuckles, so I have reported the car to the police. In this garage we have a zero tolerance policy on violence.'

- 'We have had staff reductions here at the garage. Because of this, I haven't had time to take care of your car. But it has been here, and you must understand that we can't complete all of our assignments with the budget we have.'

- 'When I was going to start repairing the car I drove it into the garage, and on the way it started throwing engine parts around. They flew all over the place. I obviously can't have it like this at work, so I pushed the car out into the yard and called you. You must take it home. It's just a disturbance here. But I still want to be paid, since I didn't have less work to do; after all, I had to tidy up everything it had thrown around.'

We can probably quickly agree that I won't be going back to that garage again. When I leave my car at the garage I expect the mechanics to do their job and to take responsibility for the repairs. I expect them to get help if they can't do the work we have agreed on, just as I expect them to have the necessary tools and methods. Nor do I want to hear any excuses about the garage's financial situation.

THE TEACHER'S EXCUSES

Unfortunately I all too often meet teachers out in the schools who think in the same way as this mechanic. They don't understand that it is the school's and their own task to ensure that the pupils learn what they need to in order to reach the goals, manage in the educational system, and manage in life. All kinds of excuses can be heard, ranging from the pupils' poor motivation and lack of knowledge on the one hand to financial problems on the other. To place the responsibility somewhere other than on yourself and on the school in this manner is of course not acceptable. Most importantly, it means that the school will not succeed in its mission. If the school is to succeed, it must take full responsibility for the pupils learning what they should and for the pupils behaving in a way that permits learning.

There are many tools and methods embedded in the different chapters on principles in the first part of the book. In this part, I will construct a framework (evaluation tools and action plans) around these methods that will make it easier for you to take the necessary responsibility. The three scenarios described are common in schools. With their help, I will show you how you can use the principles and affect regulation model described in the first part of the book.

Summary

School can be likened to a garage intended to teach the pupils the things laid down in the learning goals, where you are one of the mechanics, or craftsmen, who do the work. But in order for this to succeed, it is important for you to understand that your work with the pupils is a form of craftsmanship and that it is your responsibility to ensure that the assignment is completed successfully.

13

Example Situations and Action Plans

THE BASIC PRINCIPLE OF BEHAVIOUR MANAGEMENT

I often find that teachers try to solve difficult situations in ways that not only take care of the situations here and now, but also make the pupil choose another behaviour next time. This is of course impossible. But it is the reason why we tell pupils off and punish them. In reality the best way to manage a situation is to make sure the situation de-escalates as fast as possible. And the best way to make the pupil choose another behaviour the next time is to change the conditions. This means that our main strategy on conflicts and acting out could be:

1. Manage the situation without escalating the situation.

2. Evaluate. What went wrong?

3. Change what needs to be changed in order to avoid repeating the situation next time.

In Part 1 of this book we looked at how to manage difficult situations, how to evaluate our expectations, and how to change what needs to be changed. In Part 2 we will look at this again, but also on how we evaluate our own behaviour in difficult situations. And we will take a closer look on changing our own behaviour. Because that's where the power is. One of the tools is the action plan.

ACTION PLANS

Action plans for conflict situations are simple lists of how to act when there is a conflict. The plans should preferably be individual in nature – in other words they should relate to a specific pupil. Some people no doubt will think that action plans are just more unnecessary paperwork, but remember that they are only needed for situations that have actually occurred, not for all those that haven't. For most pupils no written action plans are needed, for the simple reason that those pupils are not involved in conflicts that are difficult to handle.

Before you start with the action plan, you should first write down a list of warning signs for the pupil concerned – in other words, what the pupil usually does when things start to go wrong. They may talk a lot, find it difficult to wait their turn, raise their voice, or bite their fingers. It's not a matter of things the pupil does all the time, but rather behaviour that you have noticed just before a situation spiralled out of control.

It's an excellent idea to write the action plan together with the pupil if you have a good relationship. In that case you can also agree on the physical framework with the pupil.

I have several times been involved in agreeing with a pupil on where to run when things get tough, for example. We have found a safe place together, such as a climbing tree, and agreed that no adults are allowed to go near the tree when the pupil is there.

Remember that it may be a good idea to show the pupil's parents the action plan, and to ask for their input. This increases their feeling of security and confidence in the work the school is doing. In addition, the parents may have ideas that you and the school have not thought of.

A GOOD ACTION PLAN HAS FIVE POINTS

A good action plan builds on a solid foundation and has five points that you need to work through. The foundation of the action plan is as follows:

1. Make room for the pupil's own strategies for handling the situation. If this does not help, move on to Point 2.

2. Make a list of *simple* distractions that have worked before. It may be to go over to the pupil and just be there, in order to create calm with your own calm, to repeat a demand in a calm and collected way, to ask the pupil to get on with their work, or to refer to the normal structure or schedule. If this does not help or if the pupil reacts negatively to this, move on to Point 3.

3. Make a list of *active* distractions that have worked before. It may be to talk to the pupil about things they like, to joke with the pupil, or similar things. If this does not help, move on to Point 4.

4. Make a list of *strong* distractions. It may be for the pupil to run around the school, or to put a current demand to the side in order to work with something that the pupil feels confident with and likes to do, or similar things. This is done the whole time in a calm way with a focus on the pupil's self-control. If this is not enough and the pupil is approaching or already in the chaos phase, move on to Point 5.

5. Have a plan for how the situation can be interrupted. It may be by suggesting a different activity somewhere else or, if the pupil is already in the chaos phase, by getting the rest of the class to leave the room. In exceptional cases, such as during dangerous behaviour, for example a violent fight between two pupils, it may be by physically separating the pupils using movement (not holding a pupil still, which increases the level of conflict and chaos, but rather holding on to an arm and moving with the pupil's movements) and then quickly moving away again, possibly several times in succession, until the pupil starts to de-escalate.

The reason I have chosen exactly five points is that we tested this out with some teachers at a school where I worked for many years. We reached the conclusion that if you have five points you very seldom reach Point 5 before the situation has been resolved, and five is few enough points to remember. With both more points and fewer points, you more often see chaos behaviour.

ADAM

Adam is sitting in class with his 27 classmates. They are in eighth grade. In comes his maths teacher, Lisa. She puts her case on her desk and says: 'You worked so well last time, so just carry on where you left off. We'll look at some new material in about quarter of an hour.'

The pupil beside Adam takes out a maths book and gets to work. So do the 26 others in the class. But not Adam. After a couple of minutes Lisa notices that he's not working and says: 'Why haven't you taken out your book, Adam?' Adam replies: 'You didn't tell us to.'

Lisa gets angry. 'You have some cheek! Pack up your things and go to the principal's office.' Adam replies, 'How come? Why is it always me? I haven't done anything', after which he throws his things on the floor and walks out of the classroom.

Lisa sees him sitting on the swing, out in the schoolyard. After a few minutes she goes out to him and says: 'Off to the principal, now. You have to do what I tell you to. If you don't, I'll make sure you are sent home for a week, so that you can think about your behaviour. Now off with you!' Adam shouts, 'I haven't done anything! Leave me alone!', and he runs away from the school. When he goes past the bicycle stands he stops to push over some of the bicycles before running on home.

In the evening Lisa phones Adam's parents and informs them that they and Adam are to be at the principal's office for a conversation on the following day. The next day, Adam refuses to go with his parents to school, and runs away from home when it's time to leave.

DEMANDS THAT DON'T WORK

It's not so difficult to understand this situation based on the principles we have looked at earlier. Lisa takes for granted that Adam knows what she means when she tells the pupils to start working. But even though Adam has gone to school for more than seven years, he still hasn't understood that maths is something you do in a maths book. The basic problem here is that Adam has difficulties in understanding cause and effect in complex situations. This is also the reason that he doesn't understand why he should go to the principal's office, and that he says: 'Why is it always me?'

When Adam says to Lisa that she hasn't asked him to take out his book, it's absolutely true. Because she hasn't. She hasn't made the demand in a way that is understandable for Adam. Lisa then immediately assumes that he replies in the way he does because he wants to irritate her. That's why she acts in the way she does. She simply hasn't understood that Adam only behaves himself if he is able to do so.

If we look at the affect regulation model, we can conclude that Lisa's affect curve is on the way up even before Adam's is. It's her demand that he go to the principal that acts as an affect trigger for him. He doesn't understand the situation, his frustration grows, and he moves into the escalation phase. Lisa then increases the affect by going into a combined escalation phase with Adam. When Adam then does what he can to handle the situation, running out and sitting on the swing to calm down, she confronts him again and pushes the conflict to yet another level, so that Adam loses control. She forgets that Adam can't cooperate unless he is in control of himself.

Adam lacks the confidence in the school necessary to handle the situation at the principal's office on the following day, which is not surprising. His strategy – to run away again when it's time for him and his parents to go to the principal – is completely predictable and the most understandable in the situation. He does what he can to resolve the situation based on the abilities available to him.

ADAM'S CONFIDENCE IS GONE AND EVERYONE LOSES

Lisa does not win in this situation. She tries to, but since the situation ends up with Adam running home, she doesn't feel that she has won. That's why she pursues the conflict via the parents and principal. And Adam of course is not interested in losing, so he stays away. Who then is the loser? Well, they both are – Lisa who can't fulfil her responsibility to teach Adam maths, and Adam who doesn't learn any maths. The question is, who bears the responsibility for this? We have to conclude that it's Lisa. Because even if Adam had gone with his parents and had had the conversation with the principal and Lisa, Lisa's way of handling the situation has reduced the chances that he will learn what he should. No-one can expect him to have the confidence in Lisa that is a prerequisite for him to pick up the knowledge he needs. Adam learns nothing by not succeeding.

SITUATIONS WILL ALWAYS ARISE

Situations of this kind arise quite often at school. There are always teachers who misunderstand or have too high expectations of their pupils' abilities. Or else they act impulsively and primitively instead of thinking first. I have not been to a single school where this type of situation did not arise. If something similar happens at your school, it is therefore important for you to learn to understand the situation and make sure that it doesn't happen again. In the situation with Adam, one of the reasons that it develops in the way it does is that Lisa works alone in the classroom, and her version of what happened is considered of greater value than Adam's version due to the prevailing power structure in the school. If Lisa is like most of us, she also finds it difficult to admit that she's made a mistake. She will probably have a tendency to defend her actions in this situation. After all, like Adam, she has just been using solutions. The problem is that she has much greater responsibility than Adam. She should have been able to find solutions that didn't cause problems for Adam.

THIS IS HOW WE CAN MAKE SURE IT DOESN'T HAPPEN AGAIN

For you and your colleagues to have a chance to improve, there must be an opportunity to discuss this kind of situation without anyone feeling guilty or ashamed. I have seen different ways of doing this. The best, in my opinion, is for the affected pupil's teaching team to sit down after every conflict that arises between a teacher and a pupil and go through the situation, based on the affect regulation model. It may be a case of name-calling or hitting, or that the pupil has run away, thrown things or furniture around, or been turned away from the classroom. Each phase should be considered in the right order, and the questions below can be used as a starting point for the evaluation. For convenience, the affect regulation model is reproduced here (Figure 13.1).

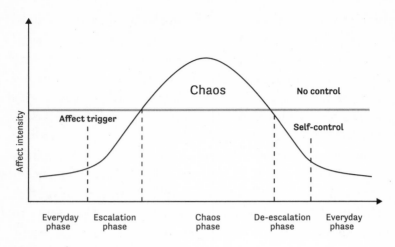

Figure 13.1 The affect regulation model

The everyday calm phase

- Who said what?

- What did the teacher expect the pupil to be able to do?

- Was the pupil able to do this?

- Were there adequate structures in place to help the pupil do what the teacher expected?

- Was the teacher's behaviour the trigger factor for the pupil's outburst of affect?

- How can we make sure that it doesn't happen again?

- Do structures around the pupil need to be changed?

The escalation phase (where the greater part of the conflict between Adam and Lisa took place)

- Which solutions did the pupil try to use?

- Were the pupil's strategies acceptable?

- Was the pupil given the chance to calm down and maintain control?

- Did the teacher use solutions that created problems for the pupil, which the pupil in turn was forced to find a solution to?

- Did the teacher increase demands on the pupil in the escalation phase?

- Did the teacher use any strategies to help the pupil maintain self-control during the escalation phase (such as creating space, avoiding eye contact, turning to the side)?

- Did the teacher instead use body language and tone of voice that reduced the pupil's possibilities to maintain control (marked and insistent body language, direct and demanding eye contact, less distance, raised voice)?

- Did the teacher use distraction strategies, such as getting the pupil to think of something else, in order to actively help the pupil to maintain self-control? (See pages 108-9 for examples of distraction strategies.)

The chaos phase (which was short in this case, at the bicycle stands)

- Was the situation dangerous?

  ▸ If it was a dangerous situation, did the teacher interrupt the situation in a quick and effective way without increasing the level of conflict?

  ▸ If it was not a dangerous situation, could the teacher have refrained from intervening?

- Did the teacher use strategies intended to avoid increasing the chaos (such as no eye contact or maintaining distance)?

The de-escalation phase

- Did the pupil get the necessary space, and some peace and quiet, in order to be able to calm down in a good way?

- Did the teacher do anything that made the situation escalate again (such as giving reprimands, acting like a foster parent, explaining the negative consequences of the behaviour, or making new demands before the pupil was ready for them)?

Back in the everyday calm phase

- Which structures must be changed in order for this not to happen again?

  - ▸ Physical structures

  - ▸ Rule structures

  - ▸ Time-related structures.

- Do you have an action plan that you think will work if the same situation arises again?

PROFESSIONALISATION – MOVING THE FOCUS FROM PERSON TO METHOD

The questions above are not very difficult to answer in Adam and Lisa's conflict. Looking through them we can establish that Lisa didn't do very much right. But since the questions are not meant to be about what the individual teacher has done wrong but about how a similar situation can be avoided in the future, the teaching team need to use them in the right way. The aim is not to single someone out, but to create preparedness for how a similar situation can be handled next time it occurs.

In educational work, this is called a professionalisation process, which means moving the focus from person to method. What is interesting here is not really why Lisa did what she did, whether it was wrong, or what the consequences should be. The important thing is what Lisa and her colleagues can do next time it happens, so that they get better at their job. For this reason, one should not talk about who is to blame for what happened, but only about the method. Preferably the discussions should result in a change to the structure of everyday life and in an action plan that everyone can follow next time a similar conflict situation occurs.

If we look at the situation with Adam and Lisa, it is quite easy to see the changes that Lisa would need to think about for next time it happens:

- If Adam doesn't take out his book, Lisa should ask him to take it out and perhaps even help him to do so in a nice way.

- Lisa should avoid being sarcastic, which increases the intensity of affect because it creates a feeling of shame in Adam.

- Lisa should put the lesson plan on the board so that Adam knows what he is going to do; it may well be over-explicit. For example: 1) work in the book on pp.47–48; 2) go through new material; and 3) work in the book on p.49.

ACTION PLAN FOR ADAM

1. Stay calm. If Adam flares up, it's often because he hasn't understood. Perhaps repeat your demand in a calm way. If this doesn't help, move on to Point 2.

2. Show the lesson structure that you have put on the board. Consider going over to Adam's desk; he likes it when you massage his shoulders for a few seconds. If this doesn't help or if he reacts negatively to this, move on to Point 3.

3. Say sorry if you've had an argument. He reacts positively to this. Ask him if he's feeling stressed and perhaps would prefer to work by himself for a while. If this doesn't help, move on to Point 4.

4. Give him the possibility to get away from the classroom, perhaps by saying that he can work in the library; he usually reacts well to this. You could give him some different, easier material that he feels confident with, such as a maths program on the computer. Keep your tone of voice calm and pleasant. If this is not enough and if he is approaching or already is in the chaos phase, move on to Point 5.

5. Let him run away – he'll be back in about ten minutes (and seldom makes trouble in other places in the meantime). Remember to text one of his parents afterwards saying that he has been for a run but that everything is OK again. They like to know.

LOUISE AND MATTHEW

It's break time at school and all the pupils are out in the playground; the weather's good. Four teachers are outside; they are standing talking to each other in pairs. Some of the pupils are playing football, some are running around and chasing each other, while others are standing talking. Matthew runs around by himself most of the time. He comes around the corner of a house at full speed and crashes straight into Louise, who is playing ball with a couple of friends. They both fall over, and Louise shouts: 'You idiot! Look, I've hurt myself. How can anyone be so stupid as to think you can run around a corner without crashing into someone?'

Matthew doesn't quite know what to say at first. He's in the class below Louise and has a bit of a crush on her. She's by far the prettiest girl in the school, in his opinion. Now he's feeling really dumb. He says: 'You didn't need to stand right at the corner. You could have worked out that you'd be standing in the way, bitch.' Louise answers: 'Don't call me bitch! You little shit!'

Now Matthew is still more unsure of the situation. He really hadn't wanted to call her bitch, it just slipped out. He tries to walk past her but she stops him, grabbing his jersey: 'And I want you to say sorry, you little shit.' Matthew struggles to get free and catches hold of Louise's hair. She screams loudly and starts kicking and hitting him with her free hand. Matthew hits back and a punch catches her right in the face.

The teachers have seen the fight and come running. One of them, Charles, takes hold of Matthew, who swings at him and catches him on the ear. Charles holds Matthew's arms but can't keep him still. His colleague Kim comes to help, laying Matthew down on the ground and holding his legs. In the meantime, Louise carries on kicking and hitting Matthew while Karen, who is Charles and Kim's colleague, shouts at her to stop. In the end Karen takes hold of Louise who is still fighting and kicking, now at Karen. Kim has to let go of Matthew's legs and holds on to Louise instead. Matthew breaks free and runs off, away from the playground. Karen, Kim, and Charles sit on Louise and Karen says: 'Now calm down. We're going to hold you until you calm down.'

SOLUTIONS THAT ESCALATE THE CONFLICT

A situation such as this is dreadful, and can have serious consequences for everyone involved. It is traumatic for both pupils and teachers. Pupils who are restrained can be badly hurt, and the risk that a teacher holding a pupil will be hurt is also high. Physical intervention increases the risk of being hurt for all concerned. At the same time it is easy to understand why the teachers on the playground in this example wanted to intervene. They couldn't just stand and watch two pupils fighting – they naturally wanted to find a solution. Unfortunately solutions often lead to escalation of the conflict instead.

START WITH CHANGES IN EVERYDAY LIFE

When evaluating situations such as the one with Louise and Matthew, it is easy to focus on the chaos situation itself. For my part, I rather think that things are less than optimal when something like this can happen at all. So instead of discussing the situation itself with the teachers, I would much rather talk to them about what changes they need to make in everyday life so that the situation does not occur again. Based on what happened between Louise and Matthew, I would like to ask Charles, Kim, and Karen the following questions:

- Was the break sufficiently structured?

- Did Matthew know what to do during his break?

- Was he running around because he didn't have the ability to structure his own time?

- Does the school have structures for where the pupils can play ball?

AVOID VIOLENT SITUATIONS IN SCHOOL

It may seem strange and unfamiliar to start at this end of a situation. If this happened to you, you would probably rather want to know how you should have handled the situation that had already arisen. The problem is that it would not have been enough to just have a strategy in place for how to separate two pupils who are fighting; it would still have been a dangerous situation. That's why it's actually more important to know how to avoid a similar situation from happening again in the future.

In school, it should really not be necessary for situations to occur that are so violent that physical intervention is necessary. That's why I prefer to avoid training teachers in the physical methods used in psychiatry and care settings. It should simply not be necessary. Instead, I usually recommend the following four simple rules for physical intervention:

- Separate pupils by keeping them moving, for example by holding on to an arm and moving with the pupil's movements. Prevent the pupil from hitting others by modifying their movements with your own, deflecting the movement sideways while moving with it, rather than opposing the movement.

- Do not use force, but movement. If you resist, the situation will escalate.

- Follow the pupil and go where they want to go, not hold them back.

- Let go of the pupil within ten seconds.

Remember that it is important to move with the pupil's movements. Re-position rather than opposition!

PHYSICAL RESTRAINT IS NOT NECESSARY

The aim of these rules is to divert the pupils physically, not to limit their freedom of movement. Physical restraint of pupils is not necessary if you use this method. It is my firm opinion that all schools, including special schools and children's services, should have a strict no-physical-restraint policy. One might ask why we should need physical restraint in the ordinary school when there are schools and classes for pupils with serious conduct disorders that manage without. And when there are even forensic psychiatry wards that have taken away the option of physical intervention, including the use of belts. To use physical restraint in schools is simply unnecessary and dangerous and should not be allowed to happen.

AFTER A SERIOUS CONFLICT

It is also relevant to discuss how to help a pupil to calm down after a fight, as in the situation above. Some schools use a mediation procedure where the two pupils who have been in a fight are put in the same room to talk about the situation. In my experience, this is only a good idea if both are well-functioning pupils. If either or both of the pupils have a hard time seeing their own role in the conflict, then the conflict will continue into the mediation procedure and neither of those involved will feel that it has been resolved. Often this corresponds to the parents saying 'Now shake hands', which probably a lot of us experienced as children. Most pupils who are involved in conflicts have a lot of conflicts going on at the same time, but they seldom take them personally and seldom bear a grudge. They are used to not understanding what is going on, and often carry on the next day as if nothing happened. And we must understand that this is OK.

COMIC STRIP CONVERSATIONS AS A METHOD

When pupils feel that a situation is unfinished, you can sit down and evaluate it together with them. One possibility is to draw the succession of events like a comic strip, with speech and thought bubbles. Then you talk to the pupil about what they were thinking in the situation and what they thought the other pupil was thinking. Most pupils get a better understanding of the other pupil's actions after going through the situation in this way. The method is called comic strip conversations and was developed by the American teacher Carol Gray.

As a teacher, you no doubt want the mediation or conversation after a fight to have an educational function: you want the pupils to learn something from what happened so that they don't end up in the same situation again. There is therefore a big risk that you will try to appeal to the pupils, or to make them feel ashamed about the conflict. We have already talked about appealing as something that is used when one has expectations that are too high for a pupil's ability to understand cause and effect. The result is that the responsibility is placed on the pupil, which is seldom effective. Shaming someone is just as ineffective.

For your work to be efficient, it is above all necessary for there to be a good relationship between you and the pupil, and for the pupil to want to maintain it at all costs. This is unfortunately something that seldom characterises the relationship between a challenging pupil and the pupil's teachers, and extremely seldom distinguishes pupils who end up in a lot of fights.

It is therefore important, when and if you intervene and then make an evaluation with a pupil, that you know the pupil well. A relationship is built on you showing that you have an interest in the pupils and their lives, but also by you joking, fooling around, and sometimes relaxing the right demands in the right situation. Just like we who have kids do with our own kids. It is also a good idea not to be too secretive about who you are. Children feel greater confidence in adults who tell them about their everyday life outside of school.

HELP THE PUPIL LAND

A good way to help a pupil calm down after a conflict is to create an opportunity for them to withdraw and be alone for a while, or to suggest a group activity that the pupil likes. You need not worry about increasing the risk of new fights by initiating relationship-building actions that feel good for the pupil (from a behaviouristic perspective – you do not reinforce negative behaviour by helping a pupil to calm down in a good way). Pupils who fight have far too many negative experiences associated with the fights they've been in; they don't really want to fight – they want to behave themselves. But to fight is most likely the most logical and understandable thing for them to do in some of the situations they end up in.

THE MOST IMPORTANT THING IS
TO PREVENT CONFLICTS

If we now return to the situation with Louise and Matthew with the knowledge above in mind, it is clear that the most important thing for the school to do is to think about what preventative actions can be taken, both in the everyday situation and in the escalation phase. Were the teachers close enough and observant enough during the break? Could they have defused the situation if they had been a little closer to Louise and Matthew? Which divertive actions would have been effective?

To work with diversions is often quite strenuous, but at the same time a way to get to grips with everyday life. If everyday life is characterised by violent conflicts then it is difficult to get an overview of how things could be changed. In such a situation, if you start working with diversions and thereby avoid violent conflicts, it often provides both understandability and the motivation to get down to organising everyday structure at breaks, division of the playground into different activity areas, and so on.

If we go through the break situation with Louise and Matthew based on the affect regulation model, we see at once that it is primarily in the everyday phase that changes need to be made; for example:

- Create an area for ball games that doesn't border on the corner of a house.

- Ask Matthew what he wants to do during the break before he goes out. It's not a bad idea to suggest structured games and activities.

- Possibly structure Matthew's breaks completely. Many pupils, especially those in younger classes, like to know what they are going to do. Creating fixed activities and group games during the longer breaks can therefore be a good idea.

- Think about whether there are enough adults present at the breaks, generally speaking.

- Structure the work of the adults at breaks. Just acting as watch is seldom enough: active work may be needed, such as taking part in activities with the pupils who most need it, including Matthew. Start from the premise that work during breaks is also work, and not a time for small talk with colleagues.

To write individual action plans for Louise and Matthew is not relevant; their behaviour is fully understandable in the situation described. The responsibility instead falls on the school and on the teachers who have created the conditions that permit the situation to arise at all. A general action plan for teachers encountering conflicts between pupils in the schoolyard would be a better idea. Such a plan, in five points, could look something like this:

1. Approach the situation, but keep a few metres away. Often it is enough for an adult to be nearby for the situation to calm down. If this does not help, move on to Point 2.

2. Ask the pupils to separate. If this does not help, move on to Point 3.

3. Make active suggestions about what the pupils can do instead. It can be an activity that is already ongoing (ball games or the like) or a place where you know the pupil likes to be (in the library or at the computer). You or another adult can offer to go with them. You can also take out something, a ball, something to eat, or something else that acts as a powerful diversion. It is important that you keep your voice calm and pleasant and focus on the pupils' self-control. If this does not help, move on to Point 4.

4. Interrupt the situation by going between the pupils, even if they are actively fighting. Get the other pupils away to reduce the affect pressure. If this is not enough and the pupils are approaching or already in the chaos phase, move on to Point 5.

5. Only in extreme emergencies (for example, if a pupil is repeatedly hitting someone else) use physical diversion to separate the pupils. This means short interventions where you keep one of the pupils in movement for 5–7 seconds and then let go. Remember to have other adults with you and that your intervention should not be domineering or suppressive in nature. If a situation reaches this stage, you should bring it up with the teaching team afterwards, and make an evaluation of the intervention.

HARRY

It's a normal day for Class 6A, where Edith is teaching English. Harry goes to the wastepaper basket to sharpen his pencil. On the way back, he pokes Archie in the back with the sharp end of the pencil. Archie exclaims: 'Edith, Harry's poking me with his pencil.' Harry smiles, and checks to see whether Charles and Andy are looking, and have seen what he has done.

When Edith asks, 'Harry, did you do it?', Harry smiles, throws a glance at his friends, and answers: 'Of course I didn't. It's just something he's making up.'

Archie says a bit uncertainly: 'He did so. And he does it every time he sharpens his pencil.' Edith asks Harry not to do it again and then carries on teaching.

BULLYING IS A SOCIAL ACTION

This is a classic bullying situation. It is completely different in nature to the other situations described in this book, but can still be interesting to look at based on the principles in the book.

It is often difficult to understand a bully's motives without starting to think in terms of good and bad. But these terms are of course irrelevant here, since this book is about what we can do to handle different situations. So we will not discuss them. It is important, however, in a situation like the one with Harry, that we try to understand his behaviour by analysing why it may be the most understandable action for him in this situation. We also need to work out how to influence the situation by presenting Harry with alternative actions that are more understandable to him.

Almost all bullying is a social action whose value lies in the acknowledgement the bully gets from others, not really in pleasure from oppressing the one being bullied. So Harry's behaviour is actually aimed at Charles and Andy. An interesting factor in this particular situation is that Edith does not have the same standing in Harry's life as Charles and Andy do, in other words – it's not important for him to be popular with her. He never weighs in the potential negative social consequences of his behaviour for their relationship but instead smiles and lies to her face. In this social situation, where Harry prioritises social standing with Charles and Andy higher than what he can get from Edith and Archie, his behaviour actually becomes understandable. He is doing what is most understandable in the situation, just as the principle says.

Another principle described in this book is about how people behave well if they are able to do so. One could argue that it does not apply in this situation. I am sure, however, that Harry is doing the best he can in the circumstances. His ability to reach social standing in a more socially acceptable way is probably low. In addition, his ability to foresee the long-term effects of his behaviour is probably limited. Harry, then, is doing what is most understandable in the situation, based on the abilities available to him.

That Archie has a problem is clear. Unfortunately Edith doesn't notice this in the current situation. She will though, if in the future she does not demonstrate greater engagement and if the bullying continues. Harry, on the other hand, has no problems with his own behaviour and therefore no incentive to change his behaviour. If the situation is to change, Edith must start to take responsibility and get involved; this is the only way to make a difference.

PUNISHMENT SPOILS THE RELATIONSHIP WITH THE PUPIL

A conversation between Edith and Harry would probably not have any effect whatsoever. Harry's respect for Edith is already fairly low, and an appealing conversation or one with threats of punishment would only worsen their relationship. Punishing Harry by sending him home for a week, or the like, would have the same result. It would also reduce his chances of achieving the learning goals. A telling-off from Edith would be even more counter-productive; it would result in Harry either ignoring her or going into conflict with her. Edith simply must find a solution that will not be a problem for Harry (or Archie).

Once again, it's about taking action during the everyday calm phase of the affect regulation model. In the situation with Harry, this means that Edith could do the following:

- Put Harry in a different place in the classroom so that he doesn't need to walk past Archie when he goes to sharpen his pencil. This is only a very small part of the whole solution since the bullying probably goes on in other places as well.

- Place Harry, Charles, and Andy in such a way that there is no immediate way of communicating between them, not even glances or the like. It's a good idea to keep them apart when dividing the class into groups or half classes.

- Create activities where both Archie and Harry can raise their social standing among their comrades. Let them do something they are good at that the others respect.

- Create structures for the breaks that protect Archie and give both him and Harry something to do that they can overview. By no means do they need to be involved in the same activities, and it's a good idea to break up the interplay between Harry, Charles, and Andy.

- Create clear rule structures together with the pupils about what bullying is and about it not being socially acceptable. It's important not to be too ambitious, though; hierarchies are normal among pupils, especially boys. This is not something you need to change. It is the injurious behaviour you want to get at, and therefore the rules must be about specific types of behaviour that are not acceptable. Forget woolly thoughts about everyone's equal value. The Swedish Board of Education's evaluation of the anti-bullying programmes used in Swedish schools in 2011 showed that none of them had any positive effect. Most of them were in fact focused on talking about everyone's equal value and getting this to work in everyday life. It's easy to think that this would be good, but unfortunately it doesn't seem to work. Remember also that there must not be consequences built into the structure, because they have a tendency to reinforce negative behaviour. In other words, one should not have a rule such as 'anyone calling other people names has to tidy the classroom'. This spoils the alliance. In addition, the pupils very seldom feel that it is a fair consequence.

- Be present and personal in the interplay with the pupils. Show an interest in their personal lives, show who you are, and allow yourself to mirror their feelings. If you can, work with a twinkle in your eye. Disinterested teachers don't connect well and don't build up the relationships with the pupils that are necessary to prevent behaviour that challenges.

- Create a structure for your own behaviour when bullying is discovered. It must not include reprimands (they unfortunately have no effect) or punishments (which don't have any effect either), but you could for example say: 'I saw what you did, Harry. Archie, I noticed. But carry on working now.' A couple of days later you could once again revisit the subject of bullying on a general level. Harry learns nothing from confrontation; by giving his behaviour the minimal attention it deserves instead, it will receive lower social power.

- Be on the look-out to see if the bullying continues. If it does, the school must make bigger changes, such as perhaps moving Harry. Not as a punishment, but in order to break the social ties that are maintaining the bullying.

ENGAGED ADULTS ARE IMPORTANT

As mentioned, an evaluation of all structured anti-bullying efforts in Swedish schools in 2011 showed that none of them had any effect. There are no shortcuts in the form of anti-bullying ambassadors, anti-bullying material, or manual-based conversation groups that work. The only thing that is effective is engaged adults who are close to the pupils and who break up negative group processes when they occur. The responsibility must lie with the adults in the school. Only then can we be sure that we will have the possibility to make the changes that are necessary.

As described earlier, the school is like a garage and we working there must do our utmost to fulfil our assignment – which is to create the right conditions for learning and to ensure that all pupils reach the learning goals.

14

Go For the Ball, Not the Player!

DON'T FOCUS TOO MUCH ON BEHAVIOUR

I would like to round off the book with a final brief reflection on the school's commission. Up to this point I have assumed that the teacher's focus is on teaching, and that we are sometimes at a loss when the assignment suddenly changes into handling behaviour that challenges.

Sometimes, however, I have encountered something completely different: teachers who are so clearly focused on behaviour that challenges that they sabotage the teaching. We have used many different methods in schools over the years. They have included environmental therapy, systematic thinking, solution-focused teaching, applied behavioural analysis, and most recently, Ross W. Greene's collaborative problem solving. All well and fine. All the different ways of thinking and working have had something to offer and they have led to various changes, although some have contributed more than others. In this book I offer yet another effective way for you to think and work.

But if, as a teacher, your social or treatment perspective is so strong that it feels more important than the teaching, then you have a problem. I have seen special schools and classes for children with special needs or conduct disorders where it was said that first the right conditions for teaching had to be created, using various methods, before the 'real' teaching started. They spent a lot of time together with the pupils, went on trips, climbed and paddled canoes for several years, and then suddenly discovered that they had never arrived at the teaching.

This is one of the greatest betrayals imaginable for pupils with special needs. Research has shown that for pupils with poorer chances of managing in society than others, perhaps due to being taken into custody by social authorities, ADHD problems, or the like, the absolutely most important factor for how the pupils manage later in life is whether they learn what they should at school.

A Swedish project called SkolFam has shown that society makes a great deal of money from a very small investment if they map out special education needs in risk groups and provide support where necessary (not a different school but rather one to two hours of support a week for one to two years). The group they looked at were pupils placed in foster homes, and the project discovered that what paid off for society was not social efforts but rather that the pupils learnt what they should.

FOCUS ON LEARNING

Because of this I have yet another basic principle that applies to all efforts in schools: 'Go for the ball!' In other words, always focus on what is important. By this of course I don't mean that you should ignore behaviour that challenges and that you should not focus on how to handle it. But you must be aware that you are not handling a pupil's behaviour that challenges for the sake of the school, but for the sake of helping the pupil to achieve the learning goals.

BEHAVIOUR THAT CHALLENGES SHOULD BE MANAGED, NOT TREATED

The school must learn to handle behaviour that challenges in a way that is simple, effective, careful, and human, so that the pupils learn more easily and are better equipped to manage in society. That is why as a teacher you should have a management focus rather than a treatment focus when it comes to handling pupils' behaviour. It is not the work you do with behaviour that challenges that will have the greatest positive effect in the lives of your pupils but rather the work you do to ensure they meet the learning goals.

In my opinion, all the things done in schools that reduce the pupils' chances to learn are awful, for example sending them home, punishing them, sending them to the principal's office, sending them out into the corridor, ignoring whether they are getting on well, and turning a blind eye to bullying. We can do better than that!

For the pupils to develop, it is necessary for them to learn the things they should; this is the commission and the responsibility that society has placed on you and the school. And to fulfil that commission you must be good at handling the behaviour that arises, and at creating the right conditions to ensure that behaviour that challenges will be as rare and mild as possible.

I hope that this book will contribute to achieving this!

Part 3

Extra Materials

Study Materials

I'm glad that you're interested in looking in more depth at the knowledge on which this book is based. In my meetings with teachers, they have often expressed an interest in study materials that they can use as the basis for discussions around the various problems they encounter.

So for this book, I have put together some materials that can work as the basis for a series of short discussions in the staff group, where you can talk about the principles presented in the book. Take, for example, 15 minutes to half an hour during each workplace or teaching group meeting and work slowly through the book. Talk, discuss, and share experiences related to the questions and problems described in the book.

Good luck!

PART 1: PRINCIPLES

Chapter 1: Always Identify the One With the Problem

Much of what you see as behaviour that challenges is only problematic from your own point of view. The pupils see it rather as a solution. This means that the pupils are seldom as motivated to change their behaviour as you are that they should do so. The pupils can sometimes also react very negatively when you indicate that you think their behaviour is a problem.

Discuss

- Think of some examples of situations where something that you considered behaviour that challenges was definitely not seen as behaviour that challenges from the pupils' point of view.

- Were there situations where this difference in point of view was instrumental in leading to an escalation of the conflict?

Chapter 2: Kids Do Well If They Can

Ross W. Greene's statement is widely known and has been used in many contexts. It mainly means that if pupils don't behave, you have probably placed too high demands on them.

The list below is one that I have constructed myself. It describes various abilities where the demands that you make on your pupils are probably often too high:

- The ability to calculate cause and effect in complex situations

- The ability to structure and carry out activities

- The ability to remember while thinking

- The ability to resist impulses

- Stamina

- Flexibility

- Social competences
- Resilience to stress
- The ability to say 'yes'
- The ability to calm down and remain calm.

Discuss

- For which abilities have your expectations on your pupils been too high? Think of a few situations for each ability.

- Also think of a few situations where things went wrong and map out where your expectations were too high. How could you modify similar situations in the future, to enable the pupils to live up to your expectations? Is it sufficient in the specific situations you are thinking about to just modify your expectations, or is it really the whole framework that needs changing?

Chapter 3: People Always Do What Makes Sense
Discuss

- Try to think of situations that you have been involved in where you can fully understand why the pupils acted as they did.

- Then think about situations in your own life where you may have done something that those around you didn't want you to do, but which you did anyway because, for you, it was the most understandable thing to do. Was the way you acted actually the best from a long-term perspective?

Chapter 4: Those Who Take Responsibility Can Make a Difference

Discuss

- Think of situations where you have tried or are trying to shirk responsibility. Do you talk more about the home situation for certain pupils than for others? Are there pupils who you keep describing with words like 'stubborn'? Are there pupils who you think should go to a different school?

Chapter 5: Children Learn Nothing from Failure

Discuss

- Think of situations that you have handled based on the notion that pupils learn from failure. How much does this idea mean for your everyday life?

Chapter 6: You Need Self-Control to Cooperate with Others

This principle is best discussed together with the next one.

Chapter 7: Everyone Does What They Can to Maintain Self-control

Discuss

- Think of situations where what you consider to be behaviour that challenges is actually the pupils' strategy to maintain self-control. What does this insight mean for your work in the future?

Chapter 8: Affect Is Contagious

Discuss

- Think of situations where your pupils are being or have been infected by your affect. It could be anger or anxiety (stress), but also joy and enthusiasm. It's a good idea to pick something positive, but also examples of where things went wrong and maybe even ended in catastrophe.

- Then see if you can think of cases where you were so infected by your pupils' affect that you lost your overview of the situation and your ability to keep the situation under control.

- Discuss possible strategies for protecting yourself from this risk.

Chapter 9: Conflicts Consist Of Solutions *and* Failures Require an Action Plan

Discuss

- Think of situations where conflicts between you and the pupils have had the structure described by the principle. Try to find both situations where you won and where you lost.

- Also think of situations where conflicts between one pupil and another have taken this course. How could you intervene in a good way in this type of situation? Try to be specific, relating in concrete terms to the situations you have thought of.

Chapter 10: Teaching is Making Demands that the Pupils Would Not Have Made on Themselves – In a Way that Works

Discuss

- Which methods do you use in everyday life to get your pupils to say 'yes'? Feel free to use the methods listed in the book (page 97), but think of your own as well.

- Which diversionary tactics do you use? It's a good idea to talk about a specific pupil, to write down the diversions you use or have used, and to share with each other.

Chapter 11: You Become a Leader When Someone Follows You

Discuss

- What do you do in order to get the pupils to give you authority? Do you have any concrete strategies?

PART 2: CASES AND ACTION PLANS

Chapter 12: It's the School's Responsibility to Ensure that the Pupils Achieve the Learning Goals

Having reached this far, it may be a good idea to go back to the principle of responsibility.

Discuss

- How well does the garage metaphor fit with your work? Do you have a tendency to:
  - ▸ place the responsibility on the pupil's family?

▸ place the blame for the pupil's lack of success on their unwillingness to cooperate?

▸ think that the pupil is not doing their best in the circumstances?

▸ use methods you feel secure with even though you have been advised that the pupil needs different methods? Could you find a way to get a clearer structure?

Chapter 13: Example Situations and Action Plans

For this chapter you will find materials for discussion in the scenarios and action plans included in the main text.

Chapter 14: Go For the Ball, Not the Player!

The last principle is probably the hardest one to talk about.

Discuss

- Think of situations where, as teachers, you have had too little focus on reaching the learning goals you are meant to be striving for with your teaching. Don't base the discussion on individual pupils where this has been a general problem, but rather on various different situations.

- Think of situations where you have invested in social initiatives, done with good intentions, but which may have resulted in the learning goals taking a back seat.

Further Reading

In this section, explanations, suggestions for further reading, and the background to the thoughts and methods described in the book are presented chapter by chapter. This is the simplest way to do it and makes the principles' overall context and connections clearer, but at the same time it means there are occasional repetitions, which I hope you will forgive.

PART 1: PRINCIPLES

Introduction

In the introduction we introduce the idea that children shouldn't learn to obey, but to be independent and autonomous. Alfie Kohn wrote that in the book:

> Kohn, A. (2006) *Unconditional Parenting: Moving from Rewards and Punishments to Love and Reason.* New York: Atria Books.

Chapter 1: Always Identify the One With the Problem

This chapter is based on thinking introduced by Andrew McDonnell in his book:

> McDonnell, A. (2010) *Managing Aggressive Behaviour in Care Settings.* London: Wiley.

And on my book:

> Elvén, B.H. (2010) *No Fighting, No Biting, No Screaming: How to Make Behaving Positively Possible for People with Autism and Other Developmental Disabilities.* London: Jessica Kingsley Publishers.

Chapter 2: Kids Do Well If They Can

The quote 'Kids do well if they can' is from Ross W. Greene's book:

> Greene, R.W. (2014) *The Explosive Child: A New Approach for Understanding and Parenting Easily Frustrated, Chronically Inflexible Children.* London: Harper Paperbacks.

If you want to learn more on executive function you can read:

> Gazzaniga, M.S., Ivry, R.B., and Mangun, G.R. (2013) *Cognitive Neuroscience.* New York: Norton.

Greene keeps an updated reference list on his website:

> www.livesinthebalance.org

The list of skills we often place high demands on is our own. But there is a lot to read on every skill:

The ability to calculate cause and effect in complex situations
You can find a lot of both research and theory on the subject
of *central coherence*; for example:

> Happé, F. (2013) 'Weak Central Coherence.' In F.R.
> Volkmar (ed.) *Encyclopedia of Autism Spectrum Disorders.*
> New York: Springer.

The ability to structure, plan, and carry out activities

> Gazzaniga, M.S., Ivry, R.B., and Mangun, G.R. (2013)
> *Cognitive Neuroscience.* New York: Norton.

The ability to remember while thinking

> Baddeley, A. (2007) *Working Memory, Thought, and
> Action* (Oxford Psychology Series). Oxford: Oxford
> University Press.

The ability to restrain impulses

> Gazzaniga, M.S., Ivry, R.B., and Mangun, G.R. (2013)
> *Cognitive Neuroscience.* New York: Norton.

Stamina
A great popular science article:

> Lehrer, J. (2009) 'Don't: the secret of self-control.'
> *The New Yorker*, 18 May. www.newyorker.com/
> reporting/2009/05/18/090518fa_fact_lehrer.

The ability to be flexible
An older defining article:

> Scott, W.A. (1962) 'Cognitive complexity and cognitive
> flexibility.' *American Sociological Association 25*, 405–414.

Social abilities

Frith, U. (2003) *Autism: Explaining the Enigma*. London: Wiley.

Resilience to stress

If you really want to understand stress, I recommend that you read Chapter 4 in:

Elvén, B.H. (2010) *No Fighting, No Biting, No Screaming: How to Make Behaving Positively Possible for People with Autism and Other Developmental Disabilities*. London: Jessica Kingsley Publishers.

The ability to say 'yes'

DiStefano, C., Morgan, G.B., and Motl, R.W. (2012) 'An examination of personality characteristics related to acquiescence.' *Journal of Applied Measurement 13*, 1, 41–56.

The ability to calm down or to remain calm

Diekhof, E.K., Geier, K., Falkai, P., and Gruber, O. (2011) 'Fear is only as deep as the mind allows: a coordinate-based meta-analysis of neuroimaging studies on the regulation of negative affect.' *Neuroimage 58*, 1, 275–285.

Sjöwall, D., Roth, L., Lindqvist, S., and Thorell, L.B. (2013) 'Multiple deficits in ADHD: executive dysfunction, delay aversion, reaction time variability, and emotional deficits.' *ournal of. Child Psychology and Psychiatry 54*, 6, 619–627.

4

Chapter 3: People Always Do What Makes Sense

You can read about how physical environments affect behaviour in:

> Norman, D. (1988) *The Psychology of Everyday Things.* New York: Basic Books.

On structure as a tool:

> Kabot, S., and Reeve, C. (2012) *Building Independence: How to Create and Use Structured Work Systems.* Lenexa, KS: Autism Asperger Publishing Co.

Chapter 4: Those Who Take Responsibility Can Make a Difference

The quote is adapted from:

> Weiner, B. (1995) *Judgments of Responsibility: A Foundation for a Theory of Social Conduct.* New York: Guilford Press.

Dave Dagnan's work:

> Dagnan, D., and Cairns, M. (2005) 'Staff judgements of responsibility for the challenging behaviour of adults with intellectual disabilities.' *Journal of Intellectual Disability Research 49*, 1, 95–101.

In this chapter we write about punishment. Maybe we need to clarify that we use the term punishment as it is used by most people. We don't use it as it is used in behaviouristic theory. If you want to read more on the negative effects of punishment you can read:

> Gershoff, E.T. (2002) 'Corporal punishment by parents and associated child behaviors and experiences: a meta-analytic and theoretical review.' *Psychological Bulletin 128*, 4, 539–579.

Shutters, S.T. (2013) 'Collective action and the detrimental side of punishment.' *Evolutionary Psychology* *11*, 2, 327–346.

Sigsgaard, E. (2005) *Scolding: Why It Hurts More Than It Helps.* New York: Teachers College Press.

On legitimising effects:

Gneezy, U., and Rustichini, A. (2000) 'A fine is a price.' *The Journal of Legal Studies 29*, 1, 1–17.

On why we punish even if it doesn't work:

Boyd, R., Gintis, H., Bowles, S., and Richerson, P.J. (2003) 'The evolution of altruistic punishment.' *Proceedings of the National Academy of Science USA 100*, 6, 3531–3535.

de Quervain, D.J.F., Fischbacher, U., Treyer, V., Schellhammer, M., *et al.* (2004) 'The neural basis of altruistic punishment.' *Science 305*, 1254–1258.

In this chapter we even write about token economies and rewards. The text should not be perceived as a general critique of behaviourism. It is an evaluation of a specific method that unfortunately often fails. Some references:

Deci, E.L., Koestner, R., and Ryan, R.M. (1999) 'A meta-analytic review of experiments examining the effects of extrinsic rewards on intrinsic motivation.' *Psychological Bulletin 125*, 6, 627–668; discussion 692–700.

Grolnick, W.S. (2003) *The Psychology of Parental Control: How Well-Meant Parenting Backfires.* Mahwah, NJ: Erlbaum.

Lepper, M.R., Henderlong, J., and Gingras, I. (1999) 'Understanding the effects of extrinsic rewards on intrinsic motivation – uses and abuses of meta-analysis: comment on Deci, Koestner, and Ryan.' *Psychological Bulletin 125*, 6, 669–676.

Chapter 5: Children Learn Nothing from Failure

The chapter is based on the article:

van Duijvenvoorde, A.C.K., Zanolie, K., Rombouts, S.A.R.B., Raijmakers, M.E.J., and Crone, E.A. (2008) 'Evaluating the negative or valuing the positive? Neural mechanisms supporting feedback-based learning across development.' *The Journal of Neuroscience 28*, 38, 9495–9503.

Chapter 6: You Need Self-Control to Cooperate with Others

Kaplan and Wheeler's original article:

Kaplan, S.G., and Wheeler, E.G. (1983) 'Survival skills for working with potentially violent clients.' *Social Casework 64*, 339–345.

Our model was first published in:

Elvén, B.H. (2010) *No Fighting, No Biting, No Screaming: How to Make Behaving Positively Possible for People with Autism and Other Developmental Disabilities.* London: Jessica Kingsley Publishers.

Other selected readings:

Diekhof, E.K., Geier, K., Falkai, P., and Gruber, O. (2011) 'Fear is only as deep as the mind allows: a coordinate-based meta-analysis of neuroimaging studies on the regulation of negative affect.' *Neuroimage 58*, 1, 275–285.

Sjöwall, D., Roth, L., Lindqvist, S., and Thorell, L.B. (2013) 'Multiple deficits in ADHD: executive dysfunction, delay aversion, reaction time variability, and emotional deficits.' *Journal of Child Psychology and Psychiatry 54*, 6, 619–627.

Wendy Grolnick's work on control, structure, and autonomy you can find in:

Grolnick, W.S. (2003) *The Psychology of Parental Control: How Well-Meant Parenting Backfires.* Mahwah, NJ: Erlbaum.

Chapter 7: Everyone Does What They Can to Maintain Self-control

Elvén, B.H. (2010) *No Fighting, No Biting, No Screaming: How to Make Behaving Positively Possible for People with Autism and Other Developmental Disabilities.* London: Jessica Kingsley Publishers.

A great popular science article on lying:

Bronson, P. (2008) 'Learning to lie.' *New York Magazine.* http://nymag.com/news/features/43893.

Chapter 8: Affect Is Contagious

The concept of affect contagion comes from:

Tomkins, S. (1962) *Affect, Imagery, Consciousness: Volume I.* London: Tavistock.

Tomkins, S. (1963) *Affect, Imagery, Consciousness: Volume II. The Negative Affects.* New York: Springer.

Tomkins, S. (1991) *Affect, Imagery, Consciousness: Volume III. The Negative Affects: Anger and Fear.* New York: Springer.

Scientific basis:

Hatfield, E., Cacioppo, J.T., and Rapson, R.L. (1993) 'Emotional contagion.' *Current Directions in Psychological Science 2*, 3, 96–99.

A great popular book on the subject is:

Nathanson, D.L. (1992) *Shame and Pride: Affect, Sex, and the Birth of the Self.* New York: Norton.

The mirror neuron research:

Rizzolatti, G., and Craighero, L. (2004) 'The mirror-neuron system.' *Annual Review of Neuroscience 27*, 169–192.

The Daniel Stern quote is from a talk he gave at the conference *Meeting of Minds* in Herning, Denmark, in 2007.

The strategies for lowering the affect are from the low-arousal approach. You can read more on that in:

Elvén, B.H. (2010) *No Fighting, No Biting, No Screaming: How to Make Behaving Positively Possible for People with Autism and Other Developmental Disabilities.* London: Jessica Kingsley Publishers.

McDonnell, A. (2010) *Managing Aggressive Behaviour in Care Settings.* London: Wiley.

Chapter 9: Conflicts Consist Of Solutions *and* Failures Require an Action Plan

Scientific documentation on restraint-related deaths:

Aiken, F., Duxbury, J., Dale, C., and Harbison, I. (2011) *Review of the Medical Theories and Research Relating to Restraint Related Deaths.* Lancaster: Caring Solutions (UK), University of Central Lancashire.

Lieberman, J.L., Dodd, C.J., Moynihan, D.P., Domenici, P.V., *et al.* (1999) *Improper Restraint or Seclusion Use Places People at Risk.* United States General Accounting Office, Report to Congressional Requesters.

Nunno, M.A., Holden, M.J., and Tollar, A. (2006) 'Learning from tragedy: a survey of child and adolescent restraint fatalities.' *Child Abuse & Neglect 30*, 1333–1342.

Paterson, B., Bradley, P., Stark, C., Saddler, D., Leadbetter, D., and Allen, D. (2003) 'Deaths associated with restraint use in health and social care in the UK: the results of a preliminary survey.' *Journal of Psychiatric and Mental Health Nursing 10*, 3–15.

On how a decrease in restraints decreases injuries:

Holstead, J., Lamond, D., Dalton, J., Horne, A., and Crick, R. (2010) 'Restraint reduction in children's residential facilities: implementation at Damar Services.' *Residential Treatment for Children & Youth 27*, 1–13.

Chapter 10: Teaching is Making Demands that the Pupils Would Not Have Made on Themselves – In a Way that Works

Martha Nussbaum's thoughts on autonomy:

Nussbaum, M.C. (2007) *Frontiers of Justice: Disability, Nationality, Species Membership* (The Tanner Lectures on Human Values). Boston: Harvard University Press.

On violence towards the one who sets limits:

Bjørkly, S. (1999) 'A ten-year prospective study of aggression in a special secure unit for dangerous patients.' *Scandinaviam Journal of Psychology 40*, 1, 57–63.

On diversion:

Elvén, B.H. (2010) *No Fighting, No Biting, No Screaming: How to Make Behaving Positively Possible for People with Autism and Other Developmental Disabilities.* London: Jessica Kingsley Publishers.

McDonnell, A. (2010) *Managing Aggressive Behaviour in Care Settings.* London: Wiley.

Smith, R.E. (1973) 'The use of humor in the counterconditioning of anger responses: a case study.' *Behavior Therapy 4*, 4, 576–580.

On how to get a 'yes':

Elvén, B.H. (2010) *No Fighting, No Biting, No Screaming: How to Make Behaving Positively Possible for People with Autism and Other Developmental Disabilities.* London: Jessica Kingsley Publishers.

On validation:

Deci, E.L., Eghrari, H., Patrick, B.C., and Leone, D.R. (1994) 'Facilitating internalization: the self-determination theory.' *Journal of Personality 62*, 119–142.

Chapter 11: You Become a Leader When Someone Follows You

Hobbes' thoughts on power are from:

Hobbes, T. (1651/1982) *Leviathan.* London: Penguin Classics.

Rawls' thoughts are from:

Rawls, J. (1971) *A Theory of Justice.* Cambridge, MA: Belknap Press of Harvard University Press.

Martha Nussbaum's thoughts on autonomy:

Nussbaum, M.C. (2007) *Frontiers of Justice: Disability, Nationality, Species Membership* (The Tanner Lectures on Human Values). Boston: Harvard University Press.

PART 2: CASES AND ACTION PLANS

The model builds on:

Kaplan, S.G., and Wheeler, E.G. (1983) 'Survival skills for working with potentially violent clients.' *Social Casework 64*, 339–345.

Whitaker, P. (2001) *Challenging Behaviour and Autism: Making Sense, Making Progress.* London: National Autistic Society.

The model was first published in:

Elvén, B.H. (2010) *No Fighting, No Biting, No Screaming: How to Make Behaving Positively Possible for People with Autism and Other Developmental Disabilities.* London: Jessica Kingsley Publishers.

The plans are based on a Swedish project:

Björne, P., Andresson, I., Björne, M., Olsson, M., and Pagmert, S. (2012) *Utmanande Beteenden, Utmanande Verksamheter.* Malmö: Stadskontoret.

You can read more on physical interventions in:

McDonnell, A. (2010) *Managing Aggressive Behaviour in Care Settings.* London: Wiley.